Strategic Intentions:
Managing knowledge networks for sustainable development

Heather Creech and Terri Willard

IISD
International Institute for Sustainable Development
Institut International du Développement Durable

The International Institute for Sustainable Development contributes to sustainable development by advancing policy recommendations on international trade and investment, economic instruments, climate change, measurement and indicators, and natural resource management. By using Internet communications, we report on international negotiations and broker knowledge gained through collaborative projects with global partners, resulting in more rigorous research, capacity building in developing countries and better dialogue between North and South.

IISD's vision is better living for all—sustainably; its mission is to champion innovation, enabling societies to live sustainably. IISD receives operating grant support from the Government of Canada, provided through the Canadian International Development Agency (CIDA) and Environment Canada, and from the Province of Manitoba. The institute receives project funding from the Government of Canada, the Province of Manitoba, other national governments, United Nations agencies, foundations and the private sector. IISD is registered as a charitable organization in Canada and has 501(c) (3) status in the United States.

Published by the International Institute for Sustainable Development

Copies are available for purchase from IISD.

National Library of Canada Cataloguing in Publication Data

Creech, Heather.

Strategic intentions

Includes bibliographical references.

ISBN 1-895536-48-0

1. Sustainable development. 2. Knowledge management.
3. Information networks. I. Willard, Terri, 1971-
II. International Institute for Sustainable Development. III. Title.

HC79.E5C72 2001 363.7 C2001-911752-3

International Institute for Sustainable Development

161 Portage Avenue East, 6th Floor
Winnipeg, Manitoba
Canada R3B 0Y4
Tel: +1 (204) 958-7700
Fax: +1 (204) 985-7710
E-mail: info@iisd.ca
Internet: http://www.iisd.org

Strategic Intentions was designed by Donald Berg.

Printed by Unigraphics Manitoba Ltd. (http://www.unigraphics.mb.ca/),
Winnipeg, Manitoba.

Acknowledgements

We are grateful for the support we have received from the following organizations:

International Development Research Centre

Canadian International Development Agency

Our work for the United Nations Environment Programme Division of Technology, Industry and Economics, and for the World Bank Institute on the Global Development Learning Network also allowed us to test much of our research on communications, structure, governance and evaluation.

We would like to thank all of our partners in the Sustainable Development Communications Network, the Trade Knowledge Network and the Climate Change Knowledge Network, as well as the many organizations we came to know through the Global Knowledge Partnership.

The following colleagues and friends have been instrumental in developing the ideas in this book:

Renald Lafond, Robert Valantin, Terry Smutylo, Katherine Morrow, Bill Singleton, Yves Petillon, Jacqueline Aloisi de Larderel, Joan Hubbard, Erik Johnson, Fiona Peterson, Dagmar Ledl, Peter Ballantyne, Grant Ballard-Tremeer, Bill Glanville, Victoria Kellett, Aaron Cosbey, Mark Halle, Jason Switzer, Scott Anderson, Carolee Buckler, Victoria Cole, Stephan Barg and Deborah Bakker.

Special thanks are due to Stuart Slayen, publishing manager, IISD, and the IISD accounting staff from whom we learned much about managing internal business processes in networks.

Table of Contents

Chapter 1
Key Messages

This book is the result of five years of experimentation with networks at the International Institute for Sustainable Development. Our early efforts with our partners were in response to the promise of technology. We explored how to bring the messages of Southern-based organizations to broader attention through the Internet. We used Web technology to aggregate the knowledge bases of our partners. And we learned how electronic communications could support collaboration across regions and sectors.

But in the past two years, our understanding of networks has grown beyond the technology that supports them. Our research has taken us into strategic communications and the effective engagement of decision-makers. We have investigated private sector experience with alliances to improve our own relationships management. We have come to value the potential of networks to foster changes in policy and practice, supportive of sustainable development, beyond what any single institution would be able to accomplish. And we have chosen to focus on one model—the formal knowledge network—as being particularly effective in moving the sustainable development agenda forward.

This book is written for practitioners who are working with different models of individual and institutional collaboration. We have tried to capture the details of network operations and management: what it really takes to help knowledge networks achieve their potential.

For those readers who are just becoming interested in how knowledge networks function, we present below our key messages.

- Most knowledge networks are initiated through the efforts of one or two lead organizations. Before bringing a network together, the lead organization should ask the following questions:
    - What is its intention in setting up the network? What policy or practice does the lead organization want to change?
    - Are partners needed to move that change forward, and if so, why? Will they contribute knowledge, or legitimacy, or access to decision-makers, or access to funding?
    - What advantage, if any, will the lead organization lose or gain by not working in a network with others? Will partners water down rather than strengthen its efforts?

In answering these questions, the lead organization can begin to define the strategic intentions of the network.

- Throughout the book, we refer to "the network advantage."
    - Knowledge networks emphasize joint value creation by all the members within the network (moving beyond the sharing of information to the aggregation and creation of new knowledge).
    - They strengthen capacity for research and communications in all members in the network. An underlying premise of a knowledge network is that the whole is greater than the sum of the parts. However, a significant benefit of participating in a knowledge network is that each of the parts becomes stronger.
    - Finally, knowledge networks identify and implement strategies to engage decision-makers more directly, linking to appropriate processes, moving the network's knowledge into policy and practice.
- The lead organization should not treat a knowledge network as a single project among many other projects to which it may be committed. These networks are complex, institutional relationships that require regular attention to be effective. Organizational management skills are essential for building and maintaining networks. These are working networks: they need structure, work plans, timelines and deliverables. And they need decision-making mechanisms among the partners for choosing and approving areas of work, research results, and funding proposals for further work.
- Networks require a network manager. To run the network efficiently, the manager cannot just be someone with a substantive interest in network activities. The manager is in effect a business process manager, whose role is to ensure that the network is implementing its work plan. The manager monitors network activities against objectives.
- Communications and engagement strategies are essential. From the beginning, network members must build relationships with those they seek to inform, influence, and work together with for change. The network must constantly look at how it will move its knowledge not just outward to broad audiences, but directly into practice.

- More research is needed to develop simple but effective means for evaluating networks. A network needs to be able to determine what changes it has effected through its research and communications work. It needs to monitor whether it is fully realizing its potential. This requires evaluation methods that not only assess individual activities, but provide some means for identifying changes as a result of its combination of efforts. We provide in the last chapter our experimental framework for network evaluation. However, we recognize that there is much more work to be done in this area.

There are many others exploring the potential of networks to fast track sustainable development. Our primary influences have been:

- the International Development Research Centre's Pan Asia Networking program, with its dual focus on infrastructure and knowledge sharing among institutions;
- the Canadian International Development Agency and the United Nations Development Programme's work with internal thematic networks;
- the World Bank's knowledge for development initiatives, in particular the Global Knowledge Partnership, the Global Development Network and the Global Development Learning Network, each of which has a different project development, management and governance structure, customized to meet the needs of the individual networks;
- Accenture's work on strategic alliances in the private sector;
- Wolfgang Reinicke's work on global public policy networks; and
- Bellanet and the Royal Melbourne Institute of Technology's work on virtual collaboration.

Five years ago, we all started with the promise of technology and learned its strengths and limitations. We now need to learn how to make and keep our promises to other institutions around the world, to work together toward sustainable development.

Chapter 2
Operating Principles

Introduction

Networks are broadly understood to be a "combination of persons [or organizations], usually dispersed over a number of geographically separate sites, with appropriate communications technology."[1] Researchers are beginning to investigate the value of network models as a means to change public and private sector actions to be more supportive of sustainable development. But networks often seem to fail to fulfill their promise. Research may be carried out and members may meet from time to time to exchange experiences. At the end of the day, however, there is often no indication that the interaction added value to individual research projects, no project collaboration by two or more members in the network, and no demonstrable sign that decision-makers read or used the research and advice emerging from the networks.

We believe that there is a fundamental deficiency in the current practice of networking. The deficiency lies in the limited understanding about how to conceptualize, develop and follow through on the strategic intentions of a network.

The way to address this deficiency is to approach networking not just to strengthen knowledge management and sharing among members, but also to actively engage the relevant decision-makers. There is a need to be more strategic in the choice of partners and in the management of the way they work together in order to keep the network focused on both its research objectives and its messages to decision-makers. There is a need to reduce the transactional costs of collaborative work that often delay the attainment of the network's intentions. And finally, there is a need to find new ways to monitor network efficiency and effectiveness.

This book describes the formal knowledge network, one model of networking in which we have observed greater emphasis on strategic intention. We see in this model a more structured and outcome-oriented approach than some other models for collaboration. The ultimate purpose of these networks is to foster change in specific policies and practices to support sustainable development. An underlying premise of a knowledge network is that the whole is greater than the sum of the parts. A significant benefit of participating in a knowledge network is that each of the parts becomes stronger.

Formal knowledge networks hold a particular advantage over other individual or collaborative approaches to change because:

- they emphasize joint value creation by all the network members (moving beyond the sharing of information to the aggregation and creation of new knowledge);
- they strengthen capacity for research and communications for all members in the network; and
- they identify and implement strategies to engage decision-makers more directly, moving the network's knowledge into policy and practice.

IISD coordinates three formal knowledge networks: the Trade Knowledge Network (TKN); the Climate Change Knowledge Network (CCKN); and the Sustainable Development Communications Network (SDCN). Over 120 researchers and interns at 40 organizations in 18 developing and transitional countries and seven countries in the North work together to address a number of critical issues in sustainable development.

- The TKN strengthens research capacity among a group of Southern-based organizations, to better assess the linkages between trade and environment, and improve the understanding in the North of Southern trade issues. Members hold in-country workshops with key decision-makers, to engage them directly in the review of the research and the formulation of recommendations.
- CCKN members undertake policy research on key themes such as vulnerability and adaptation, renewable energy and the Kyoto mechanisms. A principal activity is the training of African and Latin American delegates in the substance and process of the negotiations on the Framework Convention on Climate Change. The network has been approached by distance learning specialists to develop online versions of the training program and handbook, for broader use.
- SDCN members aggregate their individual sustainable development knowledge bases; and research and apply new approaches for communicating knowledge. The SDCN has played an important role in bringing the views of young communications professionals from the South into the G8 consultation process on bridging the digital divide between North and South.

In this chapter, we briefly examine the following:

- the drivers behind the growth of interest and experimentation with networks;
- the different types of knowledge and their relevance for knowledge networks;
- the range of collaboration models available for sharing, aggregating and creating knowledge;
- the formal knowledge network as a separate and distinct approach;
- the operating principles for formal knowledge networks; and
- a synopsis of the basic components of formal knowledge networks.

Drivers behind the emergence of networks

Networking has been in existence from the day that people began to create organizational structures. Networks and networking continue to serve as a means of sharing information for competitive and cooperative reasons among organizations and individuals with common interests. In the last 10 years, however, there has been a surge of experimentation with network models for fast-tracking sustainable development. Several factors have motivated this rapid evolution of network activity.

A significant driver has been the emergence of information and communications technologies (ICTs) in the 1980s and 1990s. ICTs have made it possible for individuals in networks to exchange information, work collaboratively and share their views more broadly. There are, however, stronger and more important drivers behind individuals and organizations making use of the technologies to create networks:

Sense of urgency

All sectors and regions have recognized "the growing complexity and inter-relatedness of major social, economic and environmental problems"[2] and "the failure of narrow approaches to solve some of the more pressing issues of poverty alleviation, environmental degradation and social breakdown."[3] New models are needed to catalyze and fast-track innovation, research and development, and the realization of economic, environmental and social benefits.

Sense of frustration

In public and academic institutions, there is a growing concern about the marginalization of many research endeavours and the lack of impact that research, in particular scientific research, has had on public policy.[4] As was noted in the 1996 report, *Connecting with the World* by the Maurice Strong Task Force, "the problem is not always a lack of information...the problem is inadequate capacity to...translate it into useful policy and appropriate action."[5] Networks have the potential to achieve a critical mass of expertise and have more influence than individual institutions can bring to bear on policy development.

Openness to private sector experience

Public sector and civil society organizations are intrigued with private sector experiments in "knowledge management" as an integral part of organizational efficiency. Knowledge management has been defined as "effectively connecting those who know with those who need to know, and converting personal knowledge into organizational knowledge."[6] The private sector upsurge in network models, strategic alliances and B2B (business-to-business) applications would not have developed without having gone through knowledge management processes—coming to an understanding of core competencies and sources of expertise within individual enterprises. Only with that understanding does it become possible to find complementary sources of expertise in other enterprises. Public sector and civil society organizations are now going through similar exercises to define who they are and what they do. And, as they come to better understandings of how to undertake knowledge management within their organizations, they have begun to ask questions about how to connect internal knowledge systems in one organization with systems in other organizations. They are learning to use these systems and processes not only to manage what they know, but to create and share new knowledge with others, and put that knowledge into action.

Explicit, tacit and implicit knowledge

Some clarity is required in our use of the term "knowledge," in relation to "information." There is a rich debate in knowledge management literature on the distinctions among explicit, tacit and implicit knowledge. Most explanations revolve around what can be written down or made explicit in some fashion, and what cannot easily be recorded or shared.[7] However, few explanations in western management literature bring into the debate cultural backgrounds, values and perceptions. We have, therefore, based our understanding of explicit, tacit and implicit knowledge upon the distinctions developed by Bellanet[8] as the most appropriate for the international sustainable development network context.

Explicit knowledge (that which is written down, recorded or codified in some manner) is often used almost interchangeably with information in the knowledge management/knowledge network context. The mapping and sharing of knowledge focuses primarily on individual explicit knowledge and its relation to organizational explicit knowledge (often referred to as "corporate memory"). In moving towards collaborative work processes, organizations often begin with knowledge mapping or knowledge elicitation, reviewing the intellectual capital of the organization (reports, manuals, etc.), identifying expertise within the organization, identifying gaps in the corporate knowledge base and recording these in a systematic way. In a network, this process of capturing and aggregating the explicit knowledge of individuals and organizations is a significant task. It creates the basis upon which a network can begin to work together.

However, our model of a formal knowledge network is grounded not just in the sharing and aggregation of existing explicit knowledge among organizations, but in the creation of new knowledge and the effective application of that knowledge. In order to accomplish all of these tasks, networks must also recognize the importance of tacit and implicit knowledge

Tacit knowledge is the understanding of how to do things. It is created by doing, by personal trial, error, reflection and revision (understanding how to research and develop new policy recommendations, learning how to run a community consultation or learning how to negotiate a policy change with a decision-maker). It is difficult, however, to articulate what that "how to" actually is. The transfer of tacit knowledge, therefore, is facilitated through shared processes (working together, mentoring and so forth) in addition to the physical transmission of written or recorded content. In a network context, creating and sharing tacit knowledge requires collaborative work techniques and the establishment of long-term relationships and trust among the participants in the network and with those who will implement the research findings.

Finally, implicit knowledge refers to an individual's "contextual surroundings…that are imbued with and shape [his or her] collective values, normative behavior, roles, customs…expectations of events"[9]—in short, an individual's culture and values. Most people understand the challenges of cross-cultural communications when bringing individuals from different organizations together in a network. More importantly, however, the network participants must also recognize the implicit knowledge norms of those they wish to influence in order to convey the knowledge from the network more effectively:

> *Social learning and effective change cannot be imposed from outside. Indeed, the attempt to impose change from the outside is as likely to*

> *engender resistance and barriers to change as it is to facilitate change. At the heart of development is a transformation in ways of thinking...*[10]

In other words, presenting a network report to a decision-maker may not have the desired effect, in part because the decision-maker has not been part of the tacit knowledge development process (learning by doing). Further, the decision-maker's own implicit knowledge (vision, values, culture) may present obstacles to the acceptance of the report's observations and recommendations. A large portion of our research on knowledge networks therefore focuses on how to engage decision-makers, how to communicate network findings more effectively and how network members can work together in order to create new knowledge and have stronger impacts and outcomes.

Different models for collaboration

The term "knowledge network" is often used as a blanket description for a variety of collaboration models. However, there are a number of important distinctions between our emerging model of a formal knowledge network and other models of institutional collaboration. There are, of course, many hybrids of these basic models, and best management practices for one model can well serve to strengthen other collaborative approaches. (See Table 1.)

Internal knowledge management networks

These networks evolve through the thematic mapping of expertise within an organization, combined with the creation of appropriate environments for knowledge sharing. Their primary purpose is to maximize the application of individual knowledge to meet organizational objectives. These networks are largely internal, although they may cross national boundaries.

Strategic alliances

In the private sector, these alliances are "long-term purposeful arrangements among distinct but related organizations that allow those firms to gain or sustain competitive advantage vis-à-vis their competitors outside the network."[11] A true adoption of the private sector model by civil society organizations would involve real value appropriation (money, time and influence) among the partners in the network. Each partner must ask itself how this alliance will further the partner's competitive advantage and strengthen its position in the marketplace of ideas. Partners do not necessarily need to have equal status in the relationship;

alliances can function with a dominant partner or partners. Strategic alliances are usually built one partner at a time.

Communities of practice

Howard Clark, in the IISD report *Formal Knowledge Networks: A Study of Canadian Experiences*, made a number of observations about "informal networks" which are relevant to communities of practice. Two or more individuals can create a community of practice for conversation and information exchange, possibly even leading to the development of new ideas and processes. Participation is purely voluntary and will wax and wane with the level of interest of the participants.[12] Communities of practice primarily build capacity. They attract individuals who are willing to share their expertise in exchange for gaining expertise from others. The principal driver is the desire to strengthen their own skills for their own objectives, more than a desire to work together on common objectives.

John Brown, in *The Social Life of Information*, makes a further distinction between communities of practice and networks of practice[13]—the latter being even more informal. Members rely largely on communicating through bulletin boards, web sites and listservs—posting information and queries but rarely interacting or collaborating directly with one another.

Networks of experts

These networks bring together individuals rather than organizations; the invitation to join is based on expertise in a particular area.

Information networks

These networks primarily provide access to information supplied by network members, occasionally with overlays of interpretative materials that organize content thematically. However, they are fundamentally passive in nature. Users must come to the network—physically or electronically—to benefit from the work of the network.

Formal knowledge networks

Formal knowledge networks tend to be more focused and narrowly-based than information networks; more cross-sectoral and cross-regional than internal knowledge management networks; more outward-looking than communities of practice; and they involve more partners than some strategic alliances. A formal knowledge network's strengths lie in its productivity and its impact on decision-makers. It is weak, however, in communicating research with broader audiences.

Table 1. Collaborative models.

Type	Group	Description
Internal knowledge management networks	Canadian International Development Agency (CIDA)	*Scope:* CIDA's internal thematic networks bring together CIDA staff throughout the organization. Each network has a specific scope of interest. Some also have work plans for research and other activities. *Membership:* CIDA staff only, however, CIDA is exploring the connection of these internal networks with external institutions, experts and networks. *Structure:* In general, ad hoc committee structure. *Communications:* Internal to CIDA only.
	United Nations Development Program (UNDP): Global Hub/SURF system	*Scope:* Tracks the expertise of staff in the UNDP field offices around the world. *Membership:* UNDP staff only. *Structure:* Managed through a central computer portal and e-mail query system. *Communications:* Internal to UNDP only.
Strategic alliances	Global Responsibility and the International Institute for Sustainable Development	*Scope:* An alliance to add value to Global Responsibility's Communications Platform which captures corporate social and environmental reporting, by integrating with IISD's business web site which holds tools for improving sustainable development practices in business; also to combine mutual interest in business-NGO relations. *Membership:* IISD and Global Responsibility. *Structure:* Governed by a memorandum of understanding. *Communications:* Web sites will be open to the public; annual forum with business/ NGO leaders to present and discuss issues of common concern.

Type	Group	Description
Communities of practice	SD Webworks [Initiated by IISD and the Sustainable Development Communications Network]	*Scope:* Forum on the Web to raise questions and exchange information about best practices in using electronic media to communicate sustainable development. *Membership:* Open to all interested practitioners. *Structure:* Informal. *Communications:* Interactions posted on web site, open to the public.
	Global Knowledge Dialogue (GKD) [Initiated by the Global Knowledge Partnership]	*Scope:* Forum on the Web to discuss all aspects of knowledge for international development. *Membership:* Open to all interested practitioners. *Structure:* Actively moderated. *Communications:* Interactions posted on web site, open to public.
Networks of experts	Consultative Group on Sustainable Development Indicators [Initiated by IISD]	*Scope:* The group is working to develop aggregated indices for sustainable development. *Membership:* Individual members rather than organizations; by invitation; based on their reputations and expertise in the field. *Structure:* IISD serves as Secretariat; regular meetings; regular e-mail interaction on closed list. *Communications:* Results of work posted on web site; open to the public; strategic promotion of research findings to selected key institutions (ex. UN Department for Economic and Social Affairs); interactions of the group are private.

Type	Group	Description
Information networks	Development Gateway [Initiated by the World Bank]	*Scope:* A central portal site on the Internet which links a growing number of country gateways to local development information and provides additional thematic content on a wide range of development issues. *Membership:* Organizations managing country gateways; other levels of participation under review. *Structure:* Under review. *Communications:* Gateway open to the public.
	OneWorld International	*Scope:* Full range of social justice and environmental issues. *Membership:* Network of OneWorld Centres; members of centers are non-profit organizations sharing the vision and values of OneWorld. *Structure:* OneWorld International is wholly-owned by OneWorld International Foundation. *Communications:* Web site open to the public.
	Pan Asia Networking (PAN) [Initiated by the International Development Research Centre]	*Scope:* IDRC's program is to build Internet capacity with development organizations in Asia; to provide a central portal to link member sites. *Membership:* Service partners and content partners that have been supported through IDRC grants; e-commerce partners are development organizations wishing to sell products and services through the central portal. *Structure:* Managed as an IDRC Program Initiative. *Communications:* Web site open to the public; PAN membership includes category for PAN policy-makers. These are policy-makers on ICT issues who facilitate, impact and are influenced by the work of PAN: they are part of PAN's target client group.

Type	Group	Description
Formal networks	Climate Change Knowledge Network (CCKN) [Initiated by IISD]	*Scope:* Policy research on key climate change themes such as vulnerability and adaptation, renewable energy and the Kyoto mechanisms; training in the negotiating process. *Membership:* Selected developed and developing country research institutes with expertise in climate change; by invitation. *Structure:* Governance agreement; Network Coordination Unit hosted by IISD. *Communications:* Network web site; training workshops; policy advice to target decision-makers.
	Global Development Network (GDN) [Initiated by the World Bank]	*Scope:* Support and link research and policy institutes involved in development. *Membership:* Seven regional development networks and their members. *Structure:* An independent, incorporated organization with its own board of directors. *Communications:* GDN web site and e-mail lists open to public; research competitions and development awards.
	Global Knowledge Partnership (GKP) [Initiated by the World Bank, CIDA and other organizations]	*Scope:* Brings together all organizations (including the private sector) working on knowledge for development, including innovative uses of information technology. *Membership:* Open to organizations and businesses working on knowledge for development issues; fee based. *Structure:* Executive committee elected by members; secretariat co-hosted by Malaysia and Switzerland. *Communications:* GKP Portal; annual meetings of the membership.

Type	Group	Description
Formal networks (continued)	Regional and International Networking Group (The Ring) [Initiated by IIED]	*Scope:* To promote collaborative work in sustainable development, especially on water, livelihoods, multilateral environmental agreements and trade. *Membership:* Predominantly Southern independent research and policy organizations; by invitation. *Structure:* Loose affiliation; Ring secretariat hosted by International Institute for Environment and Development (IIED). *Communications:* Selected publications accessible on IIED web site.
	Sustainable Development Communications Network (SDCN) [Initiated by IISD]	*Scope:* Integrating Internet communications strategies into broader communications strategies; increasing the quantity and accessibility of Southern knowledge on the Internet. *Membership:* Selected sustainable development organizations around the world with communications expertise; by invitation. *Structure:* Governance agreement; Network Coordination Unit hosted by IISD. *Communications:* Public portal site integrating member content; second site for posting communications training materials workshops; web site reviews.
	Trade Knowledge Network (TKN) [Initiated by IISD and the International Centre for Trade and Sustainable Development (ICTSD)]	*Scope:* Policy research on trade and environment linkages. *Membership:* Selected developing country research institutes with expertise in trade and environment; by invitation. *Structure:* Network Coordination co-hosted by IISD and ICTSD. *Communications:* Research published on the TKN section of the IISD web site; country workshops with key decision-makers; policy advice to target decision-makers.

Type	Group	Description
Formal networks (continued)	Canada's Networks of Centres of Excellence	*Scope:* Centres have been established in specific research areas, such as telelearning; sustainable forest management; respiratory health. *Membership:* Government, academic, private sector; by invitation based on research excellence. *Structure:* Usually highly structured, with a board of directors. *Communications:* The federal funding program requires the articulation of communications plans as part of the grant requirements.
	Global Public Policy Networks	A useful survey of these networks, including the World Dams Commission, the Global Environment Facility and others has been prepared by Wolfgang Reinicke, in *Critical Choices.*

Drawing from our observations, we have created a preliminary spectrum of collaboration models, ranging from networks of individuals within a single organization, to networks of many different organizations. Intersecting with this range of collaborators is the knowledge being shared and developed, from a narrow focus on single issues to a broad array of interests. The third axis on this model illustrates the range of stakeholders and audiences to be served through these models, from internal institutional interests, to targeted groups of decision-makers, to general audiences.

Figure 1. Collaboration Models.

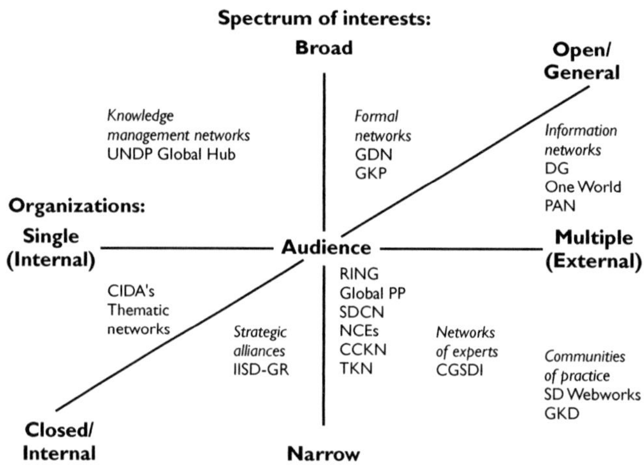

Abbreviations

CCKN: Climate Change Knowledge Network

CIDA: Canadian International Development Agency

CGSDI: Consultative Group on Sustainable Development Indicators

DG: Development Gateway

GDN: Global Development Network

GKD: Global Knowledge Dialogue

GKP: Global Knowledge Partnership

Global PP: Individual Global Public Policy Networks

IISD-GR: International Institute for Sustainable Development and Global Responsibility

NCEs: Networks of Centres of Excellence (Canada)

PAN: IDRC's networking program in Asia

SDCN: Sustainable Development Communications Network

TKN: Trade Knowledge Network

The formal knowledge network and its operating principles

Our primary interest lies close to the intersection in Figure 1 of members, interests, and audiences. These are the networks with narrower scopes of interest, more limited membership, and with highly targeted audiences for the outputs of their work.

For example, IISD has brought together 10 organizations in the Trade Knowledge Network (TKN): eight from developing countries, plus the International Centre for Trade and Sustainable Development in Geneva and IISD.The network has been established to build the base for effective policy input on trade and environment issues at national levels. The members all have significant expertise in researching national and international trade policy. Built into the design of the network is the requirement for partners to hold in-country workshops with key decision-makers, to engage them directly in the review of the research and the formulation of recommendations. The TKN emphasizes peer review of country-level research, to strengthen network-wide understanding of national and regional issues, complementarities and variations in the policy environment of each member. Technical support has been provided to improve members' electronic communications capability, so that they can share their knowledge more broadly. At the international level, its members are collaborating on equipping developing country policy-makers to strengthen their voices on sustainable development-related issues in the World Trade Organization. The TKN demonstrates the network advantage: the joint value creation through peer review and collaboration on policy and advice; capacity development on research and communications; and the emphasis on the strategic engagement of specific decision-makers.

We believe that these formal networks have the potential to have real influence with decision-makers, if their strategic intentions are well-defined from the beginning; if they are well-structured and managed; and if they build communications and engagement into their day-to-day actions. We have developed the following working definition of formal knowledge networks:

> *A formal knowledge network is a group expert institutions working together on a common concern, to strengthen each other's research and communications capacity, to share knowledge bases and develop solutions that meet the needs of target decision-makers at the national and international level.*

The key elements in this definition focus on purpose, expertise, capacity development and the recognition that the knowledge being shared and developed is not primarily for the network itself but for use by others, specifically decision-makers.

Based on our definition, we have developed several operating principles for formal networks:

1. Knowledge networks are purpose driven.

   We have observed that the narrower the focus, the more influential a network becomes. We recommend, therefore, that institutional collaboration take place around a single issue or problem rather than a broad spectrum of interests. Focus is essential. The network's research on the issue should be transdisciplinary, always keeping in mind the sustainable development framework of economics, environment and social considerations, as well as the governance implications of its work. The purpose of the network could be thematically based (e.g., trade, dams, ozone depletion) or regionally focused (e.g., environmental policy options in Central America).

2. Knowledge networks are working networks.

   One of the greatest challenges in setting up and running a network is moving the participants beyond sharing information to actually working together on solutions. In our view, knowledge networks are far more "work" than "net." A working network is driven not just by research, but by implementation. As part of creating work plans for the network, the members should focus on how the results of the network's research will be used. The work plans should include strategies for the application of the research: How will the research be linked to the public policy process? How will the process or technology developed by the network be commercialized or put into practice by those outside the network?

3. Knowledge networks require institutional commitment beyond the participation of individuals and experts.

   While expert networks and consultative groups have their place, we have learned that a knowledge network requires the commitment of an institution for several reasons:

   - *Accountability:* The participants in the network represent institutional mandates rather than personal research interests. The agenda is, therefore, more likely to be focused on implementation. Participants are also held accountable for their work not only by their colleagues in the network, but by the institutions they represent.

   - *Continuity:* Networks can take up to a decade to thrive and have real impact. With institutional commitment, it is more likely that work will continue even if there are staff changes.

- *Commitment of resources:* The network activities will be endorsed as part of each institution's mandate, more easily justifying financial and in-kind support from participating institutions and ensuring their involvement in promoting the results of the network's research.

4. Knowledge networks are built on expertise, not just interest.

   The identification and selection of members is one of the most important tasks of the network. The reputation of the network, and the level of influence it will have, will be based on the expertise and credibility of the members. We also suggest, as a guiding principle, that institutional membership be based on expertise and the capacity to undertake the research and implement work plans. Interest in an issue is not, in itself, reason enough to include an organization in a knowledge network. Membership in a formal network should be based on merit. This lends an aura of exclusivity to network activities, which makes development workers trained in consensus and public participation methodologies uncomfortable. Nevertheless, in order for a knowledge network to create new knowledge and to have real influence, that knowledge and influence must be grounded in expertise and reputation. If exclusivity is a concern of the network, then communications mechanisms can be employed to bring points of view from outside of the immediate network membership. These include workshops, electronic conferences, the nomination of associate members for specific activities and the formation of more open, dynamic "working groups" within the formal network.

5. Knowledge networks are cross-sectoral and cross-regional.

   Knowledge networks should result in a reduction of boundaries between sectors such as universities and industry, or governments and civil society.[14] Sometimes, this can be accomplished through appointing representatives from different sectors to the network, as with Canada's Networks of Centres of Excellence. In other cases, this is accomplished by including cross-sectoral interests in work plans and implementation strategies. For example, the Trade Knowledge Network is composed entirely of policy research institutes, however, the research of the network is reviewed at country workshops attended by representatives of government, civil society and the private sector.

   International knowledge networks must include the experience of developing and transitional countries. This respect for diversity—diverse values, interests and knowledge—is the "basis for crafting creative solutions that are more likely to last."[15]

6. Knowledge networks must develop and strengthen capacity in all members.

   Strengthening capacity is critical to the formal knowledge network model. Organizations create knowledge networks to learn from each other and build on each other's strengths. Capacity development occurs at all points in the work plan: in research management; in the substantive issues; in virtual teamwork; in communicating findings more broadly; and in influencing decision-making.

7. Knowledge networks are communications networks.

   This final principle underpins all the others. The knowledge created and aggregated by the network must be shared beyond the network members. This operating principle is part and parcel of a network being a purpose-driven, working network. Mechanisms must be put in place from the beginning to reach targeted decision-makers who will be the ones to put the research of the network into action. These engagement strategies include traditional communications approaches including distributing printed reports and placing the content on a network web site. But, the strategies must go beyond that and build relationships with decision-makers through regular, repeated contact, engaging them in discussions on the research and recommendations through workshops, electronic conferences, and other means.

   Broader audiences should also be informed about the network, through effective use of web communications technologies on a network web site, and through marketing and positioning on other web sites, including the individual sites of network members, portals and gateway sites.

The relationship among these principles can be illustrated through the following nested diagram. The first two principles related to purpose and work lie at the heart of the network. The second group of principles addresses a variety of membership considerations including the composition of the network (expertise, cross-sectoral and regional experience) and the interaction of members (institutional commitments and capacity development). These serve to strengthen the reputation and effectiveness of the network, without which it would have no impact on decision-makers. The final principle, that the network is a communications network, emphasizes the *raison d'être* of the network: the transfer of its work into implementation through the engagement of decision-makers and communication with broader audiences.

Figure 2. Operating principles of formal knowledge networks.

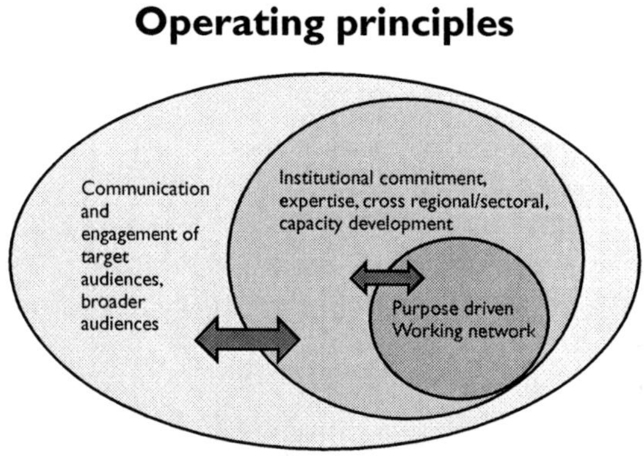

In 1996, IISD and six other organizations (five based in Southern and transitional countries and one based in the North) formed what would become known as the Sustainable Development Communications Network. The purpose of the network is to improve access to developing/transitional country knowledge on the Internet, and to strengthen the ability of civil society organizations in both the North and the South to integrate Internet communications into their communications strategies. Members undertake joint projects such as maintaining the Internet portal to the knowledge bases of member organizations (http://sdgateway.net), and the creation of more in-depth modules on common issues, such as sustainable livelihoods and public participation.

The SDCN governance agreement sets out the network objectives and the protocols for working together. New members have been brought into the network, to strengthen the network's understanding of regional perspectives on sustainable development and on web communications. This effort has led to a new network initiative to develop training materials for civil society organization web managers tasked with delivering sustainable development research on the Internet.

The SDCN has identified the Global Knowledge Partnership (GKP) and Global Development Network (GDN), both fostered by the World Bank, as the two key processes it wishes to influence. GDN representatives participated in the Web communications training initiative, in order to transfer the SDCN approaches to the communications staff of GDN members. Of greatest significance has been the SDCN's role in bringing the views of young communications professionals from the South into the work plan of the GKP and its G8 consultation process on bridging the digital divide.

Components for success

We have found that effective formal knowledge networks usually have certain components, some of which are well-understood and have been extensively documented and others which are less well-understood or previously uninvestigated. For example, while the use of ICTs to support network interactions among members and to facilitate the dissemination of information has been studied in detail, less exploration has gone into making the necessary link into the public policy process and into decision-making venues. Member relations and governance is often glossed over in the building of networks. Human resource issues have not been adequately addressed, in particular the pivotal role of a network manager. The role of young professionals in networks also needs further exploration. And, we are all chasing the chimera of evaluation: we need to better understand how to measure the outcomes and influence of a knowledge network.

External communications and engagement strategies for network audiences

According to our principles, knowledge networks need to be purpose driven, working networks, and they must be communications networks. This means that the knowledge created by the network must be for broader application outside of the network. There are two levels of audience for networks:

1. The target audience, or stakeholder group – those whom the network most wants to influence with the outputs of its work. We often prefer to use the term stakeholders, as it moves beyond the concept of a passive receiver of a message to the concept of someone with a vested interest in action.

2. Broader audiences – those individuals and organizations interested in or working on the same issues as the network.

Each network should continually ask what impact it hopes to have and on whom. The participants should identify their target audience or stakeholders with as much specificity as possible. The network should consider how it will move its advice and solutions into practice. On one level, this requires creating an effective link between the work of the network and the appropriate policy development process. On a more direct level, the network should consider engaging representatives of the target audiences more actively in the actual work of the network, to ensure better acceptance of network findings.

Communications strategies for the release of research findings to broader audiences should be developed at the same time as work plans.: Such strategies can include a network web site; print and electronic publishing; open computer conferences to discuss work; and integration with strategies for flowing the research results and recommendations into other media (print, radio, TV interviews, etc.).

A more comprehensive exploration of this component is contained in the next chapter.

Relationship building, management and governance

We are exploring the need for setting network goals and objectives (the "purpose" or focus of the network); network membership issues; governance and decision-making mechanisms; day-to-day management through a secretariat or coordinating unit; and funding and resource sharing issues. Our experience indicates that without this amount of structure, a network will do little more than exchange information from time to time. People become fascinated by collaborative technologies, but after a while the novelty wears off. The network falls into disuse without institutional commitment and staffing to continually push all of the participants. The opportunity to develop new policy recommendations and new development practices would be lost without this level of attention. As has been observed by others, these processes are two per cent technology and 98 per cent management of relationships.[16] Structure is an important support to the creation of a sense of community within a network, defining and maintaining the obligation and commitment of participants.

Further information is provided in Chapter 4.

Internal communications infrastructure and virtual teamwork protocols

For members to learn from each other and build on each other's strengths, knowledge networks require a communications infrastructure and protocols to support the joint work of network members. An important step in managing a knowledge network is the creation of a private "extranet" to link the network members. The extranet provides a common "office" for the network where members can post network documents and progress on research and meet electronically with other network members. An understanding of virtual teamwork is essential for members to interact creatively and productively within the objectives and timelines of network projects.

Chapter 5 provides more coverage of the internal communications necessary to keep networks focused on their research objectives and their messages to decision-makers.

Evaluation mechanisms

It is a common observation that what you can't measure, you can't manage. More research on measuring the overall performance of knowledge networks is required in order to manage them more effectively. We think that pooling our knowledge and staff resources in a knowledge network may result in more cost-effective research, particularly when adequately supported by information and communications technologies. Clark comments specifically on the financial health of many of the formal networks in his study of the Networks of Centres of Excellence and other Canadian networks. The success of knowledge networks should also be measured by the quality of work on the research agenda; network influence on decision-making processes; their operational performance (for example, their success in strengthening the capacity of partner organizations in research and communications); and the results of their communications strategies. Richard Stren and Janice Stein have developed a counterfactual approach to evaluating knowledge networks ("Would we know less if the network weren't in place?").[17] This approach is helpful in illustrating how a network can work to fill gaps in knowledge and innovation. IDRC's "outcome mapping" methodology may provide additional insight into the impacts that knowledge networks may have on relationships, actions and beliefs of those working within and influenced by the network.

Chapter 6 explores in more detail the options available to networks for evaluation of their work and their influence.

Additional research

Management of Web communications

The current proliferation of networks is driven in part by the availability of Web communications technologies to support the work of organizations in networks. However, it has been our observation that many current and emerging knowledge networks are still not optimizing Web communication with audiences outside of the network. We are, therefore, paying particular attention to how the Web can be used for effective audience identification, engagement and communication. We have drafted additional working papers on the tools and methods needed for communicating sustainable development on the Web and for measuring site use.

The role of young professionals

More research is needed on the minimum human resource requirements for knowledge networks. Institutional commitment is essential to ensure a constant, critical mass of researchers actively working on the network's agenda. We have also learned that there must be a network manager in place, designated to keep people interacting with each other.

However, in our working paper "Hidden Assets," (available at <http://www.iisd.org/pdf/2001/networks_youth_networks.pdf>) we focus our attention specifically on young professionals in knowledge networks. We have learned that effective networks have roles for young professionals—graduate students, interns and young employees. Young people bring fresh research perspectives, collaborative work styles and strong Internet communication skills to the network. Young professionals are in fact a significant factor in the success of a network.

Value of the knowledge network approach

The rationale for investing in knowledge management and knowledge networks,

- filling the knowledge gaps that inhibit policy development for sustainable development;
- generating recommendations that will fast track innovation for sustainability;
- resolving current frustrations with inadequate or inappropriate policy development and implementation; and
- learning from each other across sectors and regions about best practices,

has been more than adequately explored by others:

- the evaluation of IDRC's extensive network experience in the report "IDRC networks: an ethnographic perspective";[18]
- the University of Toronto study on "Networks of knowledge: development experiences in a university setting,"[19] by Richard Stren and Janice Stein;
- the UNDP's experience with establishing its Global Hub and SURF system;

- the work of Wolfgang Reinicke on global public policy networks;[20]
- the World Bank's Knowledge for Development report[21] and related suite of Global Knowledge initiatives; and
- the wealth of related literature in management journals and on the Internet.

In 1998, IISD and IDRC commissioned a study of Canadian experience in formal knowledge networks with particular interest in the model of the Networks of Centres of Excellence (NCE)—primarily a domestic model accelerating the creation of knowledge for domestic application. The resulting report by Dr. Howard Clark—*Formal Knowledge Networks*—flagged a number of innovations in the NCE model that could be used to strengthen international research, development and policy networks. Those innovations included more formal and rigorous structures and governance, the inclusion of other sectors in the networks (in particular the private sector), and the emphasis on deliverables. While Clark was particularly intrigued with the economic benefit derived from those deliverables through commercialization, the message for IISD was that a network has to have an avenue for implementation. Research networking for its own sake is no longer an acceptable *modus operandi*; it doesn't realize the potential for networks to convert knowledge into action for sustainable development.

Based on these contributions to the field of networks, and drawing from our own experience, we believe that the formal knowledge network is an excellent model for institutional collaboration and partnerships. The knowledge network approach leads to focused collaboration, better-informed research results, new knowledge and real influence.

Rather than reiterating these findings, our work looks at what we think are some of the basic building blocks for successful knowledge networks. This series is not a study of why institutions should become involved in networks, but rather a report on how to create and strengthen knowledge networks. We hope that our observations will help network managers, participants and supporters capitalize on this approach.

Evolution of IISD's interest in networks

Since its inception, IISD has functioned as a research and communications institute, engaging people of all backgrounds in producing and sharing knowledge about sustainable development. Our work is based on the ideology of partnerships—we can solve problems and maximize opportunities more effectively together than as individuals[22]—and on the ideology of information and communications: providing the right information to the right person at the right time will lead to improved decisions and actions.

The following is a brief chronology of our experiments and successes.

1991 to date

The publication of the *Earth Summit Bulletin* and its successor, the *Earth Negotiations Bulletin*—using electronic media to serve and expand audiences concerned with environment and development conventions and seeking to improve the international environmental regimes through openness and transparency of the negotiating process. IISD's Reporting Services also serves to link decision-makers with the academic sector, through creating electronic communities for discussion on key issues within individual negotiations. Most recently, Reporting Services has fostered a debate on compliance systems under the Kyoto Protocol to the UN Framework Convention on Climate Change, through the forum "Climate-D."

1992–1994

Creation and distribution of the Projet de Société database for tracking the implementation of Agenda 21 across Canada, in order to build and support a national community of interest and effort.

1993 to date

Internal experiments with Mosaic, leading to our first web sites on the Internet at the beginning of 1994. We currently attract three million users annually to our three major sites in our "web space": IISDnet (communicating the knowledge of the institute); the SD Gateway (integrating our knowledge with other leading sustainable development organizations around the world); and Linkages (our Reporting Services covering the progress of negotiations and conferences on environment and development).

1995 to date

Creation of the Consultative Group on Sustainable Development Indicators (CGSDI). The CGSDI has brought together leading experts from around the world working on aggregated indices to measure global progress towards sustainable development. The group was established by invitation, interacts via a closed electronic mailing list, and is working primarily on the creation of the "Dashboard of Sustainability"—an Internet-based interactive system to illustrate environmental, social and economic indicators.

1996 to date

In 1996, we began to build organizational networks through our Spinning the Web project. Spinning the Web started as an experiment on using technology to get more information from the South onto the Internet. It has evolved into our prototype for working with a group of like-minded organizations to integrate our knowledge bases more effectively on the Internet and to stimulate new approaches to creating and communicating sustainable development knowledge more effectively.

1996

In 1996, IISD approached IDRC and the North South Institute to champion a review of Canada's role in the world of the 21st century. Maurice Strong was asked to chair a task force of eminent Canadians from all sectors. The resulting report, *Connecting with the World: Priorities for Canadian Internationalism in the 21st Century*, focused on the need to accelerate the creation of substantive knowledge, and the need for knowledge-based networks to multiply, disseminate and expand knowledge. Equally important was the building of the capacity to use, adapt and build knowledge for sustainable development at the local level, and to build a base upon which effective and appropriate policy could be developed.[23]

1997 to date

IISD's Trade Knowledge Network was established to build research capacity among a group of organizations to better assess the linkages between trade and environment in Argentina, China, Central America, Pakistan, South Africa and Vietnam. The emphasis in the Strong Task Force report on building the base for effective policy input at the local level was influential in the design of the TKN. The TKN was, therefore, oriented to individual country studies and policy recommendations targeted at national rather than international audiences. Built into the design of the network was the requirement for partners to hold in-country workshops with key decision-makers, to engage them directly in the review of the research and the formulation of recommendations.

1998

As a follow up to the Task Force report, IISD and IDRC commissioned a study of Canadian experience with formal knowledge networks. We examined the CIDA Centres of Excellences, the Networks of Centres of Excellence, networks established with support from IDRC, and a number of NGO advocacy initiatives, such as Mines Action Canada. The resulting report, *Formal Knowledge Networks*, flagged a number of innovations in the NCE model that could be used to strengthen international research, development and policy networks.

1998 to date

Based on the findings of the Clark report and our experience with our first two networks, we established a third knowledge network_the Climate Change Knowledge Network. The CCKN blends the best features of Spinning the Web, with its emphasis on effective uses of ICTs to share an integrated knowledge base from a network of institutions, and the TKN's emphasis on policy applications. Members within the CCKN work on domestic and international climate change concerns. For example, a major emphasis has been on the training of African delegates to the Framework Convention negotiations; developing a workshop format and a supporting handbook for all developing country negotiators.

In turn, Spinning the Web has been recast into the Sustainable Development Communications Network, with a formal governance agreement and focus on joint projects and work plans across the network. The Trade Knowledge Network, in its second phase, will include more emphasis on knowledge sharing across the network in addition to its country-level work. At the international level, its emphasis will be on equipping developing country policy-makers to strengthen their voices on sustainable development-related issues in the World Trade Organization.

1999 to date

We are also experimenting with regional policy networks (RPNs). The RPNs "aim to pull together and network the key institutions and individuals within a region who have capacity in the field of sustainable development policy. In each case, a form of steering committee is established composed of leaders in the field. Their purpose is to oversee the network as a whole, select priority areas for work, and ensure the delivery of the resulting policy ideas where they will be most effective."[24] Selection of priority areas is in fact determined by whether a clear outlet for the work can be identified. RPNs are being established in Southeast Asia (anchored in Vietnam) and Central America (anchored in Costa Rica).

Endnotes

1 Clark, Howard. *Formal Knowledge Networks: A Study of Canadian Experience* (Winnipeg: IISD, 1998), p. 1.

2 The Impact Group. *Strengthening Environmental Research in Canada* (Ottawa: Discussion Paper prepared for Environment Canada, 2000), p. 19.

3 Titi, Vangile. *Building Partnerships for Sustainable Development*, Working Paper (Winnipeg: IISD, 1993), p. 3.

4 Meeting of the Canadian Environmental Sciences Network, Ottawa, January 26, 2001.

5 Maurice Strong Task Force. *Connecting with the World: Priorities for Canadian Internationalism in the 21st Century* (Ottawa: International Development Research Centre; Winnipeg: International Institute for Sustainable Development; Ottawa: The North-South Institute, 1996), p. 6.

6 "A survey of E-management," *The Economist*, 11 November 2000, p. 20.

7 Cortada, J. and J. Woods, eds. *The Knowledge Management Yearbook 2000–2001*, <http://www.cwlpub.com/nickolsarticle.htm>.

8 *Knowledge Management: Implications and applications for development organizations*, Key terms and definitions, Bellanet, <http://www.bellanet.org/km/main/glossary.html>.

9 *Ibid.*

10 Stiglitz, J. "Scan globally; reinvent locally: Knowledge Infrastructure and the Localization of Knowledge," *D+C Development and Cooperation*, No. 4, (July/August 2000), pp. 8–11, Posted at <www.dse.de/zeitschr/de400-3.htm>.

11 Jarillo, C.J. *Strategic Networks—Creating the Borderless Organization* (Oxford: Butterworth-Heinemann, 1993)

12 Clark, p. 9.

13 Brown, John and Paul Duguid. *The Social Life of Information* (Boston: Harvard Business School Press, 2000), pp. 141–142.

14 Clark, p. 2.

15 National Round Table on the Environment and the Economy. *Building consensus for a sustainable future: guiding principles. An Initiative undertaken by Canadian Round Tables.* (Ottawa: NRTEE, 1993), p. 10.

16 Regional meeting of Crossing Borders: E-governance in Canada, Winnipeg, December 2000.

17 Stein, Janice and Richard Stren. Draft. *Networks of Knowledge: Development experiences in a university setting.* (University of Toronto, 1999).

18 Bernard, Anne K. *IDRC Networks: An ethnographic perspective* (Ottawa: IDRC, 1996).

19 Stein, Stren.

20 Reinicke, Wolfgang H. *et al. Critical Choices: The United Nations, networks and the future of global governance* (Ottawa: IDRC, 2000).

21 The World Bank. *World Development Report 1998/99: Knowledge for Development.*

22 Titi.

23 Strong Task Force, p. 7.

24 Halle, Mark. *Internal briefing note on Regional Policy Networks*, IISD, 2000.

Chapter 3
Dating the Decision-makers

Introduction

The goal of communications for sustainable development is to change policy and practice—to bridge the gap between knowledge and action.

Traditionally, however, there have been only two types of "communications" strategies:

1. public relations (PR) strategies that are focused on raising or managing a positive profile for an organization or corporation; and
2. marketing strategies that "sell" a particular concept or product.

Marketing strategies are further divided into two camps: traditional *business marketing* approaches which require an analysis of customer needs, behaviour and media habits; and *social marketing* approaches which focus on behaviour change rather than sales, but still require analysis of target audience attitudes and media habits.

The traditional PR, business marketing and social marketing approaches have tended to be focused on, and worked best for "selling" single organizations, single products, or single issues to narrowly-defined target audiences. However, sustainable development is built on the cooperation of multiple stakeholders, partners, and alliances, and the intersection of multiple considerations within the spheres of economy, environment and social well-being.

Within the sustainable development community, we need to expand our views of communications in response to:

- the complexity of the issues;
- the number of groups working independently and collaboratively on the issues;
- the increase in availability of tools to support collaboration;
- the speed and penetration of today's media vehicles; and
- the changing concept of "audience" from passive recipients of products to stakeholders and partners in problem-solving.

Sustainable development organizations are increasingly shifting their focus from developing communications strategies to instituting *engagement* strategies. Engagement is a process of relationship-building that acknowledges the power of two-way communications. It is a process of moving people from being recipients of information to being partners in the process of developing new solutions. It is a process of joint learning which blurs the distinctions between communicator and audience, effectively reducing the role of much traditional communications theory and language about target audiences and market segments.

Audiences and partners will vary depending on the topic addressed, but may include individuals from governments, businesses, community organizations, and the financial community. Sustainable development communicators must utilize a suite of tools and approaches to ensure that decision-makers are:

- aware of critical sustainable development issues;
- knowledgeable of possible solutions/approaches; and
- confident in their ability to invest in/develop/modify solutions for use in their own situations.

This chapter focuses on the particular challenges of developing and implementing engagement strategies in the context of formal knowledge networks. In addition to outlining the theoretical basis for engagement strategies, it provides practical advice on the development and implementation of engagement strategies in network contexts.

Theoretical basis for engagement strategies

Fundamental to the engagement approach is an understanding that in creating behavioural change, relationships are more leveragable assets than information. The real problem isn't that people don't have access to information. The problem is that once they have information they can't influence anybody.[25] Before any of us is willing to take a risk and change our behaviour, we must be confident that the advice is sound, relevant to our own situation, and that we are able to modify it to meet our needs. In a world of information overload, our primary mechanism for filtering information, assessing its trustworthiness and deciding what to act upon is our peer group.

Relationships build the trust necessary to bridge the gap between knowledge and action for sustainable development. Relationships, not information, are at the centre of all communications.

Knowledge networks focus on relationship-building with decision-makers within government, business and civil society around the world. These relationships are built, maintained and managed toward achieving concrete sustainable development goals. Since trusting relationships take time to build and maintain, it is in the interest of each knowledge network member to work in partnership with other institutions around the world that already have established relationships with decision-makers. In addition, in many parts of the world, there is great fluidity between staff within influencing institutions and decision-making positions. Therefore, building relationships with influencing institutions is critical to directly and indirectly achieving an organization's strategic objectives.

Each well-managed relationship not only helps to achieve the network's goals directly, but also provides access to additional relationships and a broader funding base. Care must be taken to ensure that time spent on managing relationships at various levels is balanced. Networks can neither afford to alienate a potential relationship nor ignore the needs and interests of its close partners and decision-makers.

The importance of relationships to opportunities for influence is not new. However, throughout the 1990s, the focus on relationships in communications was often overshadowed by the increased emphasis on information exchange. However, as the Internet matures, research is emerging on the role of information within the broader context of community formation and learning.[26] Much of this research is based on lessons derived from the fields of marketing, fundraising, knowledge management and communications.

Lessons from the marketing community

The field of marketing has been shaken by the introduction of the Internet. In 1999, Rick Levine, Christopher Locke, Doc Searls and David Weinberger launched the *Cluetrain Manifesto* declaring:

> *A powerful global conversation has begun. Through the Internet, people are discovering and inventing new ways to share relevant knowledge with blinding speed. As a direct result, markets are getting smarter—and getting smarter faster than most companies. These markets are conversations. Their members communicate in language that is natural, open, honest, direct, funny and often shocking...[N]etworked markets have no respect for companies unable or unwilling to speak as they do...[But] most companies ignore their ability to deliver genuine knowledge, opting instead to crank out sterile happytalk that insults the intelligence of markets literally too smart to buy it.*[27]

The 95 theses of the Cluetrain Manifesto rattled the world of corporate marketing. Unfortunately, its implications have largely been missed in the world of not-for-profits intent on "professionalizing" their marketing approaches by adopting the techniques that leading edge corporations are now abandoning. Many continue to invest in contentless brochures and annual reports instead of directing their resources toward providing consistently valuable products and services tailored to the needs of their stakeholder groups. On the positive side, many civil society organizations around the world have never made the leap to "marketingese"; they continue to communicate through one-on-one conversations with potential collaborators and allies.

In addition to changes in tone and style, the late 1990s also saw changes to when and how marketing campaigns were conducted. Traditional marketing techniques relied on interrupting what people were doing at any given moment to convince them that they should be doing something else. However, it was becoming obvious that such a strategy was doomed to fail in the long run since the opportunity cost to people is too high. In a knowledge economy, information is freely available. The scarcest commodities are time and attention. *Interruption marketing* wastes information-seekers' time; in the meantime, information producers are never sure that they have their target audience's attention.

According to Seth Godin, the alternative is *permission marketing*, which offers people an opportunity to volunteer to be marketed to.[28] It allows marketers to calmly and succinctly tell their story, without fear of being interrupted by competitors. Permission marketing encourages consumers to participate in a long-term, interactive marketing campaign in which they are rewarded in some way for paying attention to increasingly relevant messages. Permission marketing is just like dating. Through this process, the producer and consumer gradually establish a relationship and learn more about each other. Many of the rules of dating apply, and so do many of the benefits.

According to Godin, there are five steps to dating your customer:

1. offer the prospect an incentive to volunteer;
2. use the attention offered by the prospect to offer a curriculum over time, teaching the consumer about your product or service;
3. reinforce the incentive to guarantee that the prospect remains willing to engage in further interactions;
4. offer additional incentives to get permission for more things from the consumer; and
5. over time, leverage the permission to change consumer behaviour towards profits.

Sustainable development knowledge networks could apply these principles as they strive to change decision-makers' actions. Incentives in this context would usually consist of the information itself, packaged in increasingly customized formats tailored to meet the needs of the individual. In exchange for providing more customized information, the network would request additional information about the decision-maker, moving from a simple e-mail address to include the person's name, position, country, experience and specific interests. Each time a product is requested, the knowledge network can learn more about what exactly that individual wants and needs. This allows for further innovation and development of products that meet the needs of known users who want to learn more.

For example, rather than trying to convince a government minister to change toward green taxes across the board with a single publication, permission marketing suggests that more can be accomplished by creating a series of smaller, more tailored products that can be delivered to policy-makers upon request. As the relationship is established and the network more clearly understands the decision-makers' predicaments, it should be able to help them achieve what they really want—environmental integrity, economic development and increased well-being, in this case. The curriculum then involves defining those things and showing policy-makers what types of policies and practices can actually be implemented given the constraints of the current policy arena. It may also involve, in this case, providing the appropriate government ministry with the communication strategies for changing public opinion to favour such taxes.

Lessons from the fundraising community

While permission marketing may sound calculating, such approaches are not foreign to civil society. Over the past decade, the concept of *moves management* has gained ascendancy in fundraising and philanthropic circles. Personal attention in cultivating and soliciting prospects is critical in a major gifts program.[29] Like permission marketing, the moves management process entails taking a series of steps (moves) with identified prospects. The idea is to move them from attention, to interest, to desire and back to attention. Essentially, you develop a strategy for each prospect. Then you track the progress of the relationship by planning contacts, implementing moves and evaluating the success of each move. It's a constantly changing strategy that you refine as you move along.

One of the greatest challenges of implementing moves management has been tracking relationships between organizations and individuals over an extended period of time. However, the increased power of database technologies and customized user interfaces has made it easier for organizations to track interactions with potential and current donor prospects. The Institute for Charitable Giving has even released its own version of Moves Management software based on Symantec's ACT! 4.+ contact management software.

However, collective relationship management is a resource-intensive task. While organizational efforts have made some progress toward systematizing knowledge about relationships, networks have largely not managed information about external relationships in a coordinated manner. The roots of the problem go beyond incompatible database systems and platforms. The lack of network contacts management is more closely linked to the real costs of staff time required to maintain formal systems. Databases are easily built, but staff within sustainable development organizations do not perceive significant benefits from systematically tracking their collective contacts and leads. Most staff are too busy implementing projects and fulfilling the expectations of current relationships to pursue many new opportunities or to mine data for potentially interesting new areas of work. Thus, while corporations have moved from developing internal systems management software to connecting these with those of their suppliers and customers, civil society organizations have barely begun to develop internal systems. CSOs do not have the infrastructure to grow or to spin off ideas in order to take advantage of all opportunities.

Lessons from the knowledge management community

Knowledge management practices are quickly moving from the private sector to the international development community. While experiments began within large donor organizations such as the World Bank and the Canadian International Development Agency, there is a growing appreciation of the need for development organizations of all sizes to create systems that help them to access their institutional knowledge in a timely manner.[30]

Most organizations are discovering that you cannot manage knowledge; it is too slippery, it changes too quickly. Rather than trying to database everything people know, it can often be more effective to foster communities of practice where people can find others who know what they need to know when they need it. This shifts the focus from classifying data to facilitating learning between people.

Communities of practice are also able to move beyond explicit knowledge to sharing implicit and tacit knowledge as well. Implicit knowledge deals with the contextual surroundings of an organization or community that shapes the collective expectations and values. Tacit knowledge refers to ways of doing things practised by individuals and communities. Most tacit knowledge cannot be fully articulated, if at all. Someone can explain it to you, but it takes trial and error to be able to truly understand the idea or to perform the action correctly.

Finally, knowledge management experts have rediscovered the power of stories and objects.[31] It turns out that interesting stories and things attract interesting people and conversations. We used to think that innovative people made innovative products, but the latest research at MIT indicates that innovative prototypes actually attract innovative people.[32]

Lessons from the social psychology community

But, how do people hear about innovative ideas and products in the first place? According to *The Tipping Point*, ideas, products, messages and behaviours spread just like viruses.[33] Similar to medical epidemics, a handful of special people play an important role in starting idea epidemics. They translate the message of innovators into something we can understand. They alter it in such a way that extraneous details are dropped and others are exaggerated so that the message itself comes to acquire deeper meaning. To begin an idea epidemic, the following roles and skill sets must be present in a social network:

- Mavens – These individuals are idea specialists. They are human databanks who are obsessive about details and about sharing them with others.
- Connectors – Connectors are people specialists. They know a lot of people from every possible sub-culture and niche. They have an extraordinary knack for making friends and acquaintances out of everyone from a farmer in a village in Ethiopia to vice-presidents of international banks. They act as social glue by spreading ideas around.
- Salespeople – These individuals have the skills to persuade us when we are unconvinced of what we are hearing. They are masters of the art of emotional expression and draw people into their own conversational rhythms on a completely sub-conscious level.

Pulling it together

In reviewing the experiences of various communications communities, we find that the following principles can serve as the basis for a successful engagement strategy. Such a strategy:

- has goals and a clear focus;
- acknowledges that people are the most important resource for sustainable development;
- uses tangible projects as a way of focusing conversations and attracting interesting people to learn from each other;

- bases participation on the individual's/organization's ability to fulfill specific roles in transforming innovation into general practice; and
- provides graduated steps for participation of stakeholders.

The next section explores how to put these principles into practice within the context of sustainable development knowledge networks.

Elements of engagement strategies

An engagement strategy can be thought of as a systematic approach to building action-oriented relationships over time. It provides a conceptual framework to help ensure that individual projects and communication strategies within a knowledge network build upon one another to foster collaborative learning and change.

Since 1996, the International Institute for Sustainable Development (IISD) has been experimenting with developing engagement strategies in the context of formal knowledge networks.

Stages of engagement

The stages of engagement can be thought of as levels in a pyramid, with the highest levels of engagement at the top of the pyramid. This reflects the reality that at any given point in time a broad base of support is required to support a smaller number of intense relationships. Seen from the perspective of the network, the levels move from providing general information to decision-makers to nurturing a relationship with them to undertaking joint actions. Over time, the size of the relation-

Figure 3. The engagement pyramid.

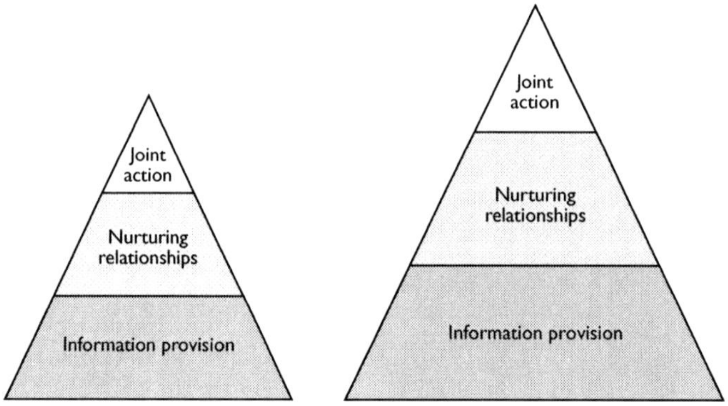

1a. Engagement pyramid – Time 1

1b. Engagement pyramid – Time 2

ship pyramid of a successful network will grow, reflecting its ability to manage relationships effectively toward achievement of network goals.

Information provision

This is the broadest type of relationship. The knowledge of the network is packaged for sharing with decision-makers. Communication strategies are planned and implemented to ensure that increasing numbers of decision-makers are aware of, and have access to, the experiences and lessons of network members. At the first level of relationship building, organizations request very little information in exchange for the provision of their knowledge base on sustainable development. However, from records of inquiries, workshop attendees, publication sales and web site statistics, the network can determine that interested individuals include a wide base of people from civil society, government, business and academia around the world.

Nurturing relationships

To grow and flourish, relationships require conversations. At some point in the provision/reception of general information products and services, either the decision-maker or the network may decide to advance the relationship. At workshops, this step is easily observed in conversations over coffee or following panel presentations. Short introductions are made and business cards exchanged. In a virtual environment, there are several ways to encourage this step to happen:

- establishment of a discussion group that opens the possibility for public conversations;
- establishment of reciprocal Web links or sharing of relevant information; and
- establishment of clear mechanisms to contact the network privately.

Following the introduction, the network and the decision-maker have time to decide whether to pursue the relationship. Too frequently, follow-up does not occur and the conversations end. To be successful, networks must ensure that follow-up occurs quickly and professionally. Since knowledge networks are distributed organizations, this requires that all members make provisions for following up on in-person and e-mail questions and feedback. Cultivation of important new contacts may require the coordinated joint actions of many members.

Nurturing relationships is a time-intensive task. It requires not just responding to conversations, but starting them as well. It requires ensuring that the network is represented at important events in order to solidify existing relationships and explore possible avenues for joint action.

Joint action

Once trust has been established and visions of sustainable development clarified, decision-makers may wish to work more closely with a knowledge network in resolving their current challenges. Joint action between knowledge networks and decision-makers usually takes the form of a funded project or consulting arrangement. Knowledge networks usually do not have adequate unallocated resources to engage in substantive joint actions without direct support from specific decision-makers. Unlike traditional development approaches, knowledge networks are usually seeking not just funding, but substantive contributions of knowledge and connections from the decision-makers as well. This is based on the understanding that decision-makers are more likely to implement policy recommendations if they have been active participants in the research.

Engagement case studies

The case studies that follow illustrate the relationships between various external communication products and services as part of a broader network engagement strategy.

Case Study I: Trade Knowledge Network

The goal of the Trade Knowledge Network is to foster long-term capacity to address the complex issues of trade and sustainable development in developing country governments, research institutions and other non-governmental organizations. It seeks to help build capacity at the national level in partner countries for stronger voices on issues of trade and sustainable development. It also seeks to help identify those areas where improved environmental protection may offer economic benefits from increased exports as well as benefits in terms of environment and development—the win-win scenarios. Finally, and perhaps most important, it seeks to bring the actual developing country experience of the trade and sustainable development linkages to a Northern audience that too often perceives those linkages through the filters of untested assumptions.

The base of its engagement strategy is the creation and provision of research reports on issues related to trade and sustainable development in developing countries. Two series of reports were created: country-specific reports and cross-cutting international issues papers on themes such as Trade-related Aspects of Intellectual Property Rights (TRIPS) and the greening of government procurement. This research is provided freely to government trade experts, academics and civil society organizations through the TKN Web site <http://www.iisd.org/tkn/> and in print publications.

Relationships with decision-makers are nurtured at various levels. While staff from various TKN member organizations interact with international policy-makers at periodic trade negotiations, the network has focused its engagement efforts on national-level trade policy-makers. To engage these individuals in issues of sustainable development, TKN members are fostering national-level networks including staff from interested NGOs, academics, businesses and government officials. These individuals are first brought together at policy workshops (or ideally, earlier during the research definition process). The goal is to help breathe independent life into these national-level networks, which can then become enduring forces for change.

While the TKN has not yet achieved a top level of engagement in terms of joint actions through the network with particular decision-makers, individual member organizations are working closely with national governments on trade policy reform. For example, the Trade and Industrial Policy Secretariat (TIPS) in South Africa hosted a workshop in July 1999 in collaboration with the Department of Trade and Industry as preparation for South African negotiations at the World Trade Organization (WTO) on the General Agreement on Trade in Services (GATS). In Pakistan, the Sustainable Development Policy Network (SDPI) has followed up its initial workshop with further meetings with officials from the ministries of environment, commerce and agriculture, especially on TRIPS-related issues. Training courses for officials have also been initiated. SDPI plans to use its good relations with the Minister of Environment to establish an inter-agency working group. This group would have monthly meetings to brief people on forthcoming issues.

The success of the network as a whole can be assessed through its ability to consciously manage relationships and meet the needs of an expanding community of developing country trade policy-makers. Over time, as the reputation of the network increases, decision-makers will move from reading TKN research results to participating in workshops to developing joint actions that change international trade policy and practice.

Case Study II: Climate Change Knowledge Network

The goal of the Climate Change Knowledge Network is to create knowledge and enhance the capacity of developing and developed countries to shape an effective, equitable and sustainable climate change regime. The network seeks to build capacity so that negotiators can take actions to link development with efforts to mitigate climate change, with sustainable development as the overall goal. In early 2000, the members of the Climate Change Knowledge Network decided to undertake an initiative to prepare African and Latin American climate change negotiators to represent their countries' interests more effectively. It was felt that many small delegations had little formal experience with either climate change issues or with strategies for managing their time and alliances during protracted negotiation sessions.

In July 2000, a five-day workshop for African negotiators was organized by IISD and Environnement et développement du tiers-monde (ENDA) in Dakar, Senegal; the three-day Miami workshop for Latin American and Caribbean negotiators was organized by the Centre for Sustainable Development in the Americas (CSDA). Following the two workshops, CSDA, with participation from IISD, ENDA and the Institute for Environmental Studies (IVM), published *"On Behalf of My Delegation,..."*, a survival guide for developing country climate change negotiators. Over 650 copies of the book and 250 CD-ROM versions were distributed at COP-6 in The Hague in November 2000. The survival guide is available online at the CCKN web site <http://www.cckn.net/delegation.htm>. The book was also translated into Spanish and French for subsequent negotiations.

By providing practical training for developing country negotiators in multiple formats, the CCKN has quickly established relationships with climate change policy-makers from around the world. Not only will this engagement strategy have short-term impacts on negotiations, but it has also opened the possibility for continued dialogue and joint action in the coming years. Some of these negotiators will likely become supporters of and participants in other network activities regarding decentralized renewable energy and vulnerability and adaptation.

Elements of communications strategies

Engagement strategies rest upon a solid foundation of expertise in research and traditional communications. For communications activities to be effective, they must deliver what a group has to say in the manner the audience wants, needs and expects to receive the message. Unfortunately, civil society organizations often focus more on their needs than those of their audiences. While they have extensive expertise in research on sustainable development topics, they have less experience with a wide variety of communications media and techniques. Publishing and communications are seen as relatively straightforward activities that any researcher should be able to successfully undertake once the research is complete. As a result, many civil society organizations develop research products and services that are written and produced in a way that they communicate most clearly only with other civil society organizations. They produce what they would like to read or see.

They may frequently be less familiar with the needs of business, government and community audiences—even though they claim to seek to influence these groups. This reduces the effectiveness of their overall work.

In order to be effective, knowledge networks must seek to build the communications capacity of member organizations to ensure that they are developing and delivering research products in the most effective manner possible. They must learn to repackage and redeliver the same information differently for different audiences.[34] The network cannot develop and deliver a communications strategy unless member organizations have some familiarity with communication practices. Participation in network activities can build on the capacity of member organizations to better manage their individual communications activities as well.

Goal-setting

Communications is a tool, not a goal in itself. The goal of any communications activity should be to change the actions or attitudes of a particular audience. Communications products and services are merely the tools to provide information, advice and expertise to people faced with decisions in order to influence them toward a desired outcome. Communications is not a value-neutral exercise.

Clear goals must include specific reference to which people one would like to take what actions within what timeframe. Greater specificity enhances a group's ability to develop products and services to meet their goals. All further decisions about audiences, communication tools and methodologies grow from that goal.

Audience identification

It may often be more efficient to target information brokers with established personal relationships with decision-makers than to target decision-makers themselves. Policy-makers, practitioners and the international development community each approach information gathering in different ways. For example, policy-makers frequently maintain contact with the academic community. Non-governmental organizations wishing to influence government policies may, at times, be more effective if they create communication products and services targeted at the academic community. Academics may then draw upon these resources in their policy-briefings for government ministers. By comparison, consulting firms often have greater legitimacy with the business community than not-for-profit organizations. Influencing senior business leaders may often be most efficiently done by providing materials to consulting firms which they may draw upon in developing training programs and consulting reports for corporations.

Understanding one's audiences includes developing an understanding of what constraints they face at any particular time. The messages developed for that audience must address how they may overcome their constraints. For example, in North America at the present time, it may not be useful to recommend raising fuel taxes to the government; it is constrained in its ability to act on the issue by public sentiment. If a group chooses to make such recommendations, they must accompany those recommendations with communications strategies and materials that the government could use to help shift public sentiment. Investing in learning more about one's audience and addressing their perceived constraints directly may increase the likelihood that recommendations are acted upon.

The selection of audience will determine the most appropriate tone and format for the communication product or service. If the desired target audience includes senior decision-makers, it must take into account their actual information gathering habits. Executive summaries and short articles in leading newspapers and magazines have a greater chance of being read than comprehensive reports. More detailed information and case studies, however, must be made available for their junior staff to review as the need arises. Young professionals in government and business play an important role in interpreting and aggregating information for decision-making. They may be more likely to seek information online through Web sites and email discussion group archives. While the style of writing must be appropriate for excerpting into policy-briefs, the design and conceptual navigation must suit the needs and understanding of the young professionals.

Ultimately, CSOs and knowledge networks must engage in "intelligence" activities to learn as much as possible about their target audiences and about other organizations vying for the target's attention and action. One's information rarely arrives in a silent vacuum. In fact, all new information adds to the clutter in decision-makers' minds and on their desks. It is increasingly difficult to design and deliver communications products that stand out from the background noise surrounding any particular audience.

Identification of appropriate tools

Civil society organizations tend to use a fairly small set of communication tools to deliver their messages to target audiences. This is usually due to a lack of familiarity with different media. Most researchers have been trained by academic institutions in the preparation of working papers and presentations. They have usually not been asked to prepare short articles, press briefs, Web modules or audio-visual materials. If the organization does not have communication staff trained in the preparation of these media, researchers resort to the techniques with which they are most familiar. Ultimately, a well-conceived communications strategy for a particular message may include many of the following tools. It is essential that the strategy be established in the project planning phase, with budget lines and responsibility for each product clearly articulated.

Personal contact

Personal contact should not be overlooked as an important communications medium. While its one-to-one nature makes it a slow way of communicating, it allows for higher levels of tailoring of messages than other techniques. In addition, higher levels of context can be established through personal contact. This significantly increases the levels of trust and the probability for action on recommendations.

Print publications

Print publications are the most common communications media used by civil society organizations. They include a wide variety of formats and lengths including brochures, editorials, journal articles, policy briefings, workbooks, newsletters, working papers and books. Some of these formats may be published by an institution; others take advantage of third party publishers. Most organizations have formal or informal guidelines for their writing, review, design, publishing and distribution. Print publications are increasingly diverging in length: short working papers that can be easily read on long flights, marked up and passed along and longer reference books. Print publications are perceived as having a high level of formality and credibility. This is due, in part, to the perceived expenses of publishing. However, as digital printing technologies spread around the globe, print publishing has become more accessible to more people. More organizations now have the ability do higher-end printing with colour, special inks, better paper, dye cutting, etc. As this occurs, print publications are becoming more numerous. In the eyes of some, this has led to a drop in the credibility and prestige of print publications. Knowledge networks, however, may reinforce the credibility of the print publications of members by serving as a form of peer review reinforcement.

Workshops

Workshops are another familiar communications tool for sustainable development organizations and knowledge networks. Workshops may be organized as stand-alone events or as part of larger international conferences. Increasingly, knowledge networks are choosing to hold workshops as part of existing conferences as a way of keeping costs under control and increasing networking opportunities. Unfortunately, in order to accommodate the ever-increasing number of organizations wishing to participate in conferences, most workshops are held in a panel format. At most, this provides 10-20 minutes for any particular presentation. This is not enough time to explore the nuances of an experience. For that reason, workshops within other conferences tend to be most useful for cementing existing relationships or for establishing new relationships. They are not very good at conveying substantive information to people with previous knowledge of the topic.

On the other hand, one- or two-day stand-alone workshops can be extremely effective mechanisms for communicating with policy-makers. Such workshops allow better targeting of participants and provide necessary time for discussion and relationship building. Other communication products can also be distributed during workshops.

Web content

The Web is an increasingly popular communications media. Given the growth of access within the academic, business, and non-profit sectors around the world, Web content can theoretically reach a broad and diverse audience. While this audience is still predominantly young and male[35], over time it is likely that a growing number of senior professionals are using the technology on a regular basis as well. In the early days of the Web (1994–1997), it was assumed that the Web was an inexpensive publishing medium. Funds normally allocated for printing and distribution could instead be invested in content development. Unfortunately, experience has shown that Web publishing is at least as expensive as print publishing. Additional expenses must be accrued for training, ongoing site maintenance and marketing. Most organizations make an initial investment in the computer and network infrastructure to control their own Web products and services. They must also invest in training staff not only in HTML coding, but also in writing for the Web, graphic design and information architecture. Given the rapid evolution of Web standards, they must also invest in redesigning existing Web content as standards and technologies evolve.

CD-ROMs

CD-ROMs have had a rough ride as a communications tool for sustainable development. While there was great enthusiasm in the early 1990s, they fell out of favour as the Web gained in strength. Today, however, CD-ROMs are seen as a useful technology for reaching organizations that may have unreliable or costly Internet access. They are also useful for users who travel frequently and may wish to browse the material from a laptop while flying to meetings. Web sites can be saved onto CD-ROMs and mailed to organizations at a low cost. While this approach does not take full advantage of CD-ROM technologies and potential user interfaces, it is cost effective. Packaging Web sites on CD-ROMs also serves as a way of familiarizing people with how to use the Web, so that they will be more comfortable with the interface and tools when they become locally available. Specialized CD-ROMs are most appropriate for training since they allow a high level of interactivity.

E-mail messages

E-mail is one of the most powerful communication tools in existence. It is the easiest way to send small quantities of information to large numbers of people around the world. According to IDC, an international technology forecaster, the number of e-mails sent on an average day was roughly 10 billion worldwide in 2000. By 2005, this will more than triple to a staggering 35 billion e-mails sent daily.[36]

However, gaining access to the e-mail addresses of individuals within your target audience can be quite expensive. To create a direct marketing mailing list requires extensive time for research on the Web. When the Sustainable Development Communications Network (SDCN) completed its online Introduction to Sustainable Development, the network co-ordination unit decided to send out a short marketing e-mail regarding the Spanish version of the module. A program assistant spent one week searching online for the e-mail addresses of Latin American professors and university departments teaching sustainable development. One hundred and thirty addresses were found in this exercise. Given the careful targeting of the recipients and the phrasing of the message and subject line, no negative feedback was received. Had the network been less careful, its reputation could have been damaged by people perceiving the e-mail message as spam.

An alternative to direct marketing is to rely upon existing e-mail discussion groups. Most sustainable development discussion groups today contain very little discussion. They serve primarily as opt-in advertising channels. Individuals subscribe in order to learn what new products and services are being developed by related initiatives. Subscribing to a small number of specialized groups is a cost effective way of reaching a large audience with a short message. There are also a growing number of institutional (e.g., IISD's New and Notable, REC Announcements, Earth Council Updates) and thematic opt-in mailing lists (e.g. Subsidy Watch, Climate-L). Knowledge networks and their constituent member organizations should co-ordinate their efforts to ensure that announcements are released in a timely manner through all related international and regional lists. If targeted, written and formatted well, list members will usually then distribute these messages to additional lists and individuals who may be interested in the subject.

E-conference interventions are another often-overlooked communications medium. Organizational and network reputations can often be enhanced by well-conceived interventions in e-mail conferences. Just as in face-to-face conferences, e-conferences provide ample opportunity for people to have a platform for sharing their own experiences. Unfortunately, many individuals do not participate significantly in e-conferences since such participation can be overlooked. However, while participation may not increase a person's standing within their own organization, it can significantly increase their reputation and ability to form alliances externally. Signature files in e-conference interventions should always indicate the person's name, job title, organization, network affiliation, e-mail address and relevant URLs. Messages should also be written in such as way that they maintain coherency if conference participants forward them to non-conference participants. While this is technically a breach of "netiquette" (Net etiquette), it happens frequently.

Theatre and the arts

Theatre and the arts are used with greater frequency and consciousness in developing countries than in industrialized regions. The field of development communications has long recognized the power of live theatre, music and the visual arts to convey important messages about environment and development. Sustainable development organizations in North America and Europe are beginning to relearn how to consciously use such techniques. Benefit concerts organized by local or regional coalitions have been dominant in this area. However, photography exhibitions and fashion shows featuring recycled clothing are also growing in popularity.

Audio and video

With the growth of broadband Internet access and media convergence, there is a growing resurgence of interest in audio-video communications. Radio, television and film are all very powerful communications methodologies. Not only are they excellent for reaching out to illiterate populations and providing training, but they are also effective conveyors of emotions and values. These are as important for influencing decision-makers as for reaching the general public. For example, IISD's video on Inuit observations of climate change in Arctic Canada has had a far greater impact on government policy-makers and the media than a working paper on the subject would have had. Images and voices from the remote Inuit community made the message of massive change more memorable than previous text-based reports from IISD.

Leveraging the media

Sustainable development organizations and networks should take advantage of media institutions and channels for sharing their research and solutions. Media events, press releases and op-ed pieces are all useful methods for communicating with the media. Media events for a knowledge network can often be planned in conjunction with network workshops or network management meetings. The SDCN was able to take advantage of the presence of most network members in Costa Rica in May 1998 to schedule a press conference with Costa Rican journalists. The Earth Council, headquartered in San Jose, Costa Rica, served as the local host and organizer. A more routine way of working with the media is the development and distribution of press releases. These can be done for new product launches; they can be especially useful if the new product launch is held as part of a larger conference. Many conferences provide a table in the media centre where conference participants may leave press releases with contact information. These press releases may lead to follow up interviews and coverage by print, radio and television journalists. Organizations such as the Institute for Media, Policy and Civil Society <http://www.impacs.org/> and the Panos Institute <http://www.panos.sn/> are growing to meet the media relations training demands of civil society organizations and networks.

Evaluation and revision

Effective communications strategies require periodic evaluation and revision. Evaluation is the measurement of results against the objectives you set during the planning process.[37] When conducting an evaluation, always consider:

- Was the development of the communications activity adequately planned?
- Did recipients of the message understand it?
- How could the communications strategy have been more effective?
- Were all audiences reached?
- Was the desired organizational objective achieved?
- What unforeseen circumstances affected the success of the program or activity?
- Did the program or activity fall within the budget set for it?

- What steps can be taken to improve the success of similar future activities?

Revision of the strategy should be based upon answers to such questions as well as updated intelligence on audience needs and desires.

Conclusion

In order to achieve any substantial impact on sustainable development policy and practice, knowledge networks must strive to maintain steady and increasing contact with policy-makers and practitioners directly and indirectly. This will require the network to make difficult choices about which relationships are most important to achieving their goals. These relationships should be actively cultivated through the use of tailored information products and services. This does not mean that other stakeholders can be ignored, however. In an increasingly interconnected world, unsatisfied non-target audiences can quickly damage a network's reputation. Therefore, networks must:

- ensure that they communicate their focus and expertise as clearly as possible; and
- cultivate relationships with other networks in order to refer less-appropriate inquiries to those who can better serve an individual's needs.

However, such activities are only fully possible within knowledge networks if the member organizations have expertise in communications and relationship management. Unfortunately, many civil society organizations do not pay enough attention to communications and relationship management activities. Knowledge networks, therefore, must explicitly address the need to build communications capacity within member networks as well as to harmonize their collective engagement efforts. If they attract funding for these activities, knowledge networks can serve as powerful mechanisms for bridging the gap between sustainable development research and action.

Endnotes

25 Manasco, Britton. “Leading Lights: Technology Designer Michael Schrage.” *Knowledge Inc.* <http://webcom.com/quantera/schrage.html>.

26 Brown, John Seely and Paul Duguid. *The Social Life of Information*. Boston: Harvard Business School Press, 2000.

27 Levine ,Rick, Christopher Locke, Doc Searls and David Weinberger. *Cluetrain Manifesto*. <http://www.cluetrain.org/> (August 16, 2001).

28 Godin, Seth. *Permission Marketing: Turning Strangers into Friends, and Friends into Customers*. Simon & Schuster, 1999.

29 Kelly, Kathleen S. “Effective Fund-Raising Management Summary” *UL-Lafayette site*. <http://www.ucs.louisiana.edu/~ksk1890/summary.html>.

30 Bellanet. *Knowledge Management and International Development*. <http://www.bellanet.org/km/> (August 16, 2001).

31 The most widely-known book on storytelling as a knowledge management practice is Stephen Denning’s *The Springboard: How Storytelling Ignites Action in Knowledge-Era Organizations*. Butterworth Heinemann: Woburn, MA, 2000. See <http://www.stevedenning.com/> for additional information and discussion.

32 Schrage, Michael. *Serious Play: How the World’s Best Companies Simulate to Innovate*. Boston: Harvard Business School Press, 2000.

33 Gladwell, Malcolm. *The Tipping Point: How Little Things Can Make a Big Difference*. Boston: Little Brown & Company, 2000.

34 While not developed in a knowledge network setting, Porter Novelli’s “Communication Strategy Statement for the National Youth Anti-Drug Media Campaign” <http://www.nida.nih.gov/rfp/5063/exhibitc.htm> is a good example of how to outline a communications strategy.

35 Pastore, Michael. “Internet Remains a Man’s Domain.” CyberAtlas. <http://cyberatlas.internet.com/big_picture/demographics/article/0,,5901_809341,00.html>.

36 IDC. “E-mail Deluge Continues with No End in Sight” <http://www.idc.com/software/press/PR/SW101000pr.stm> (October 10, 2000).

37 Ohio Arts Council. “Evaluation.” *News Media Resource Guide*. <http://www.oac.state.oh.us/resguide/evaluation.htm>.

Chapter 4
Management and Governance

Introduction

Networks are exercises in structured informality.[38]

The key principle of networking is focusing on what you do best and delegating other activities to your allies.[39]

When a group of individuals or institutions begins to set up a network, it encounters a number of creative tensions: the tensions resulting from differing organizational mandates; the tension between a closed membership and a more open network; the tension between focusing narrowly, on specific actions, and the desire to serve a broader range of interests among all of the network members; the tension between a fixed set of expectations defined by a funding proposal and the inevitable evolution of network interests which comes about through collaboration. The operational framework for a network helps to resolve these tensions, by:

- building relationships with prospective partners;
- establishing the protocols for membership and for decision-making within the network;
- setting network goals, objectives and work plans;
- specifying human and financial resource requirements and the sharing of those resources to support the network; and
- codifying these understandings in a network governance agreement.

We begin this chapter with several assumptions:

- there are one or two lead organizations championing the need for a network to achieve certain objectives that the organizations could not meet as quickly or effectively on their own;
- the lead organizations want to establish a working network rather than an information exchange mechanism; and
- sources of funding will be sought to support the work of the network. Funding arrangements may consist of:

  1. a large grant from one or two donors, to a lead institution, which then disperses funds for network projects to the members;

2. specific project grants from a variety of donors which go directly to individual members for individual projects, or to groups of members for joint projects; or
3. a combination of the two.

We examine four stages in establishing a formal network:

1. forming relationships (choosing partners);
2. organizing relationships (determining what the partners will do and how they will do it);
3. formalizing relationships (codifying network governance);
4. institutionalizing relationships (managing the internal alignment between an individual organization and the networks to which it belongs).

Other models of institutional collaboration, briefly described in Chapter 2, may be constructed and financed differently, but they are outside the scope of this discussion.

Forming relationships and choosing partners

Organizations often need a critical mass of voices in order to be heard above the cacophony of messages communicated to decision-makers every day. That critical mass can be achieved strategically through the creation of alliances and networks with other organizations. The private sector parallel is the mandate to "get big or get out." Similar forces affect civil society organizations, "which may conclude that partnerships…allow them to mount efforts collaboratively and reach a desirable scale that no one of them could achieve alone."[40] However, forming relationships with potential partners takes time. In fact, this should be considered one of the most important steps in building a network. The private sector literature on strategic alliances and networks reveals that over 60 per cent of these relationships fail outright or underperform,[41] and they fail in part because the relationships between partners were not built carefully in advance.[42] Klijn, in "Public management and policy networks," calls this process the "selection and activation of actors" within a network.[43]

Network scoping phase

The difficulty is that in the current project-driven environment for research institutes, NGOs and intergovernmental bodies, there is rarely sufficient time taken in advance to explore the common interests that will hold the network together in the longer term. A lead organization may seek preliminary consent from potential partners to create a network. Expectations for the network are then driven by the immediate objective to raise funds rather than by a careful deliberation of whether the organizations are a good "fit" with each other and whether in reality there is support for a common agenda above and beyond the sharing of financial resources raised for the network's first projects.

Every proposed network should begin with a scoping phase to explore interests and define expectations for working together. Strategic alliances in the private sector are typically built one partner at a time. With formal knowledge networks, partner organizations should be sought out with a similar commitment to the exploration of mutual interests, getting support from one organization before approaching the next, or only approaching two or three initially. A mass-distributed form letter or e-mail calling for expressions of interest in a network is not appropriate for a formal knowledge network. Contact should be made personally to each prospective partner, at two levels:

- the head of the organization
- those individuals within an organization who will be the champions and actors within the network.

It is far better to have a small number of dedicated working partners than dozens of marginally committed organizations.

In forming relationships with potential partners, one should take the time to learn how each organization works. This becomes even more important when partners represent a cross section of sectors and regions, where organizational cultures vary widely. The objective for the scoping phase is to learn which organizations and staff members will be most committed to working with the network (responsive to correspondence, willing to keep to work plans, able to promote the network within their own organization and so forth). Understanding levels of commitment will help to build a foundation of trust among the members. It will also help to reduce the transaction costs of co-managing projects across the network.

Seeking out research and communications expertise

Another oversight at the proposal stage is in placing the emphasis on the research expertise of each partner, to the exclusion of their communications capacity. The expectation is set from the beginning that the lead organization(s) will take responsibility for all of the communications functions, rather than integrating the communications and engagement strengths of each prospective partner into the network. And yet, for the network as a whole to achieve real impact, all of the partners will need to contribute their capacity to share the network research findings throughout their own spheres of influence.

In the process of learning how an organization works, one should look explicitly for those individuals who will be instrumental in the communications and engagement process. As discussed in Chapter 3, these include three specific roles:

- the mavens – the research experts;
- the connectors – those who have the connections to decision-makers that the network wishes to influence; and
- the salespeople – those who can design and communicate the messages most effectively for decision-makers.[44]

The scoping phase should also include a preliminary technical assessment of the communications capacity of potential partners. Networks are underpinned by the technology for internal communications among network partners and strategic communications to external audiences. Some capacity to participate electronically in network activities should either be present or, if not present, budgeted for as part of setting up the network.

Criteria for membership

In formal networks, the lead organization(s) should be able to justify the invitation of each member to other organizations inside and outside the network. This requires unambiguous criteria for the selection and invitation of members. Transparency to others is all the more important in a structure where core membership is restricted. In identifying potential partners, consider the following criteria:

Table 2. Membership criteria checklist.

Criterion	Rationale	Demonstrated through:
Shared commitment to sustainable development goals; complementarities of mandates; motivation for joining the network.	The goal of the network should be consistent with and further the mission of each organization entering into it. Fundamental conflict between missions works against the efficiency and effectiveness of the network. Partners need to understand the motivations of their colleagues for participating in the network, to understand what the value added is for each partner.	Conversations with key people in organizations. Talk with heads of organizations and those who will work on the network project(s).

Criterion	Rationale	Demonstrated through:
Policy research expertise: acknowledged experts within the organization.	Each organization has to have more than just an interest in the focus area of the network; it has to have real strength to do quality research on the issue. These will be the "mavens" in the network.	Print, electronic publishing record; staff reputations.
Access to decision-makers.	Each organization has to have a proven capacity to influence the policy process. Organizations have to go to the places where policy is formed and be able to access and shape the opinions of those who form it. Some part of the interaction with decision-makers can help to shape research priorities, including gaps in policy that may not yet be acknowledged. Look for the "connectors" within organizations: while they may not be directly involved in the research, they will be instrumental in moving the research into the decision-making arenas.	Participation in local processes, (workshops etc.), track record in advocacy with policy-makers, consulting work for governments.
Communications capacity.	The partners should collaborate not only on the research agenda but on the communications strategies — and they will need to bring in the advice of the communications staff within their own organizations. Look for the "salespeople": the strategies will be stronger if each partner has some capacity to provide advice and support. Also look at the technical infrastructure supporting internal and external communications.	Talk to the publishing and communications staff within the organization; learn more about their techniques and successes. A preliminary technical assessment for electronic communications capacity might also be helpful.
Sectoral representation.	Cross-fertilization of ideas is stronger when the network includes private sector as well as civil society groups; government as well as academic. The multi-sectoral composition of a knowledge network can lead to real innovation and practical implementation of policies and solutions.	Mandates of the organizations will reveal sectoral interests. If it is not possible to include other sectors in the core partnership, significant attention should be paid in the engagement strategy to reach and involve representatives from other sectors.

Criterion	Rationale	Demonstrated through:
Regional representation.	Cross-fertilization of ideas also takes place when members are drawn from different regions.	Locations of head offices, mandates of the organizations will reveal regional interests.
Size of organization; organizational priorities.	Working networks are time-consuming. The smaller the organization, the more thinly staff may be spread across projects. Networks inevitably get more limited attention when institutional priorities arise. The network then devolves to sporadic information sharing rather than real collaboration with partners.	Conversations with key people; Look for recent restructuring of the potential partner, including any change in focus; Ask what their experience has been in participating in other networks.
Financial, administrative commitment.	Ensure that funds will be spent on network activities, not channeled into other institutional activities.	Financial statements; Conversations with key people in organizations, including financial staff.
Collaborative work culture.	Internal work cultures that are innovative and that demonstrate an "ease of working across internal boundaries and high concern for people…such cultures nourish stronger relationship building skills and are more capable of adapting to others"[45] in networks and alliances.	Conversations with key people in organizations; Examples of joint projects carried out in previous partnerships.

Not every partner chosen will meet all of these criteria in whole or even in part. However, an awareness of the strengths and limitations or challenges facing participation in a network will help to mitigate and overcome obstacles to performance within the network.

Extended relationships

Accommodating donors

We have seen a number of networks wishing to include donors more explicitly in the network. In part, this is requested by the donors, who want to "learn by doing." And in part, the network itself wants to interact more closely with donors as part of engaging their interest in—and contribution to—the projects.

In the Sustainable Development Communications Network, donors are considered members of the network and are encouraged to actively learn from the SDCN's experiences by participating in network meetings and on the network extranet. Donors are invited to review and advise on network projects but not asked to take the lead on any network projects.

Extending relationships to other organizations

Formal knowledge networks are innovation networks, seeking to accelerate the creation and implementation of solutions for sustainability. While it is important to focus on the specific work plans for a network and to manage financial and human resources for the core membership, the network should not work in a vacuum from other groups interested and involved in similar work. This is a major challenge networks face time and again: how to keep the network focused on its core business and to keep the transactional costs of managing multiple relationships to a minimum while at the same time learning from others outside the network. Networks should create mechanisms to respond positively to requests for participation by non-members, to demonstrate respect for the expertise and commitment in other organizations. Networks should find means to include different ideas and perspectives in order to enrich their work. And finally, networks should build their linkages to other networks on similar issues. But this is easier said than done.

The SDCN established two mechanisms to provide opportunities for participation by those organizations interested in joining the network. One was a Web ring to link web sites of sustainable development organizations (the Sustainability Web Ring); the second was an online community of practice (the SD Webworks) for organizations to share lessons on effective communications practices, without the expectation of working together on projects within the core membership of the SDCN. These mechanisms benefited the core membership as well as the "petitioning" organizations. The mechanisms (1) served to increase the profile of organizations working on similar issues, without bringing them into the actual work of the network; (2) brought new ideas and contacts into the network; and (3) provided yet another avenue for the promotion and dissemination of the network's products.

The Climate Change Knowledge Network established an observer category to accommodate other organizations working on climate change:

> "Observer members may attend meetings of the Climate Change Knowledge Network, offer suggestions for projects, and will have access to the network members. Observer members are organizations, not individuals, that are undertaking climate change research and action relevant to the network. As observers, they are not asked to participate directly in projects but are encouraged to share relevant work. Observers are asked to cover their own costs of participation. Potential observer members must approach a network member if they wish to become an observer. The network will then accept observers based on the following criteria:
>
> - ability to provide expert advice on network projects;
> - ability to assist the network with meeting its purpose and vision;
> - ability to assist with fundraising efforts for network projects; and
> - ability to disseminate network activities to broad audiences."[46]

In keeping with the principle that these are working networks, even observers of the CCKN are expected to make an active contribution.

Sample relationship models

Note that we call these relationship models rather than membership models. They illustrate the core and extended relationships which form and evolve over time.

The Trade Knowledge Network (TKN)

In the first phase of the Trade Knowledge Network (TKN), from 1997 to 2000, IISD created a "hub and spokes" model for the network. IISD managed the daily operations of the network. Each member received funding for research on trade and environment linkages in their country. Each member held an in-country workshop with representatives from different sectors to discuss the research findings. This set of bilateral relationships did not function as a collaborative network until the end of the first phase when the results of each project were shared and lessons learned in common were identified.

Figure 4. TKN Relationships, Phase 1.

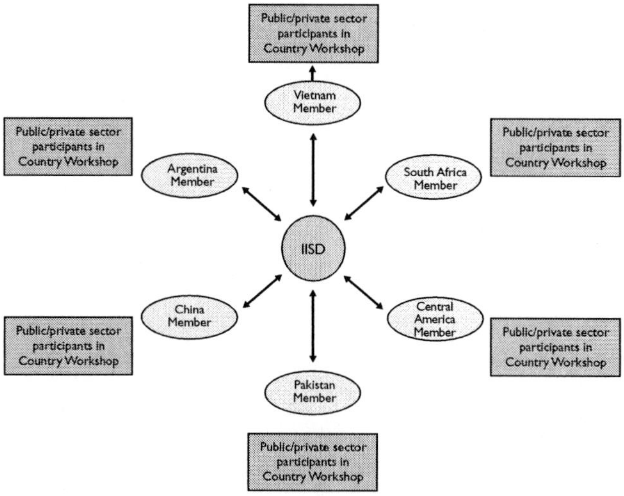

In the second phase of the Trade Knowledge Network which launched in 2001, the organizers implemented a combination of a strategic alliance, a formal knowledge network of international research partners, and multi-sectoral country networks.

The strategic alliance relationship: The TKN is now jointly managed by IISD and the International Centre for Trade and Sustainable Development (ICTSD), bringing to the process their complementary knowledge bases on trade and environment together with communications, capacity development and administrative skills. This alliance brings resources to strengthen the individual research institutions from the eight countries in the network.

The formal knowledge network: A review process has been instituted, where members review and advise on each other's research proposals and findings. Members are also expected to advise on topics and authors for thematic (cross-cutting) research. Support for collaboration is being established, through regular meetings, a listserv, and a private web site for the network.

The extended relationships: Each of the individual research institutions has significant national-level convening power. During their research, they hold policy workshops in their respective countries to discuss the projects with public and private sectors. In order to maintain cross-sectoral input to their work, a third "tier" is being included—national-level networks which are groups of interested NGOs, academics, businesses and government officials first drawn together at the policy workshops.

While the country members maintain links to national level networks, the strategic alliance maintains links to international level networks.

Figure 5. TKN Relationships, Phase 2.

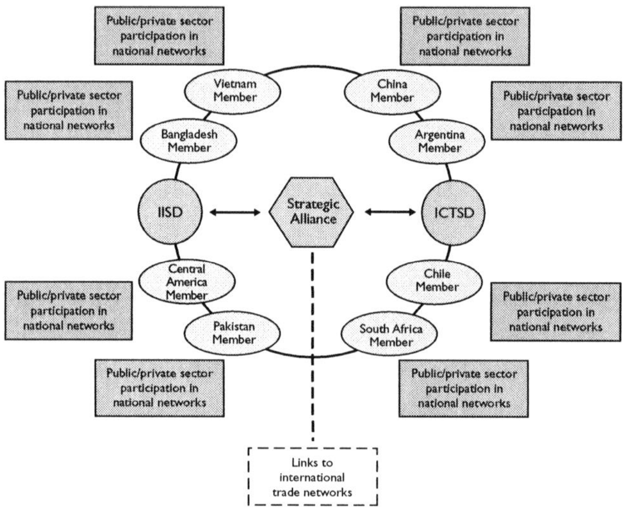

The Sustainable Development Communications Network (SDCN)

The relationships model for the first phase of the Sustainable Development Communications Network (from 1996 to 1999) also looked very much like the first phase of the TKN—IISD as the centre of the hub, with bilateral relationships with each of the members.

During the second two-year phase of the SDCN (1999-2001), it was decided that the membership should be expanded in order to increase representation from other regions of the world. New partners with complementary technical and substantive expertise were also needed to enrich the activities of the network. At the same time, the network wanted to ensure that new members understood that this was a working network, not just an information exchange network. The following accommodations were made. Three categories of network membership were created for organizations depending on the length and intensity of their working relationships with other network members:

- Founding members: seven organizations that have been involved in the original networking project since 1996. These members oversee network vision and objectives.
- Members: civil society organizations that have been active in two or more network projects.
- Affiliate members: other organizations that are approached by an SDCN member to participate in a single network project, or that approach the SDCN with a project idea of interest to at least one founding member. These members retain their affiliation with the network only for the duration of the project.

The Network Coordination Unit (NCU), based at IISD, oversees the activities of the members, ensuring that projects are completed as planned. The NCU also maintains the Sustainability Web Ring and SD Webworks. These two services provide the means for connection and interaction with organizations outside of the core membership.

Figure 6. SDCN Relationships, Phase 2.

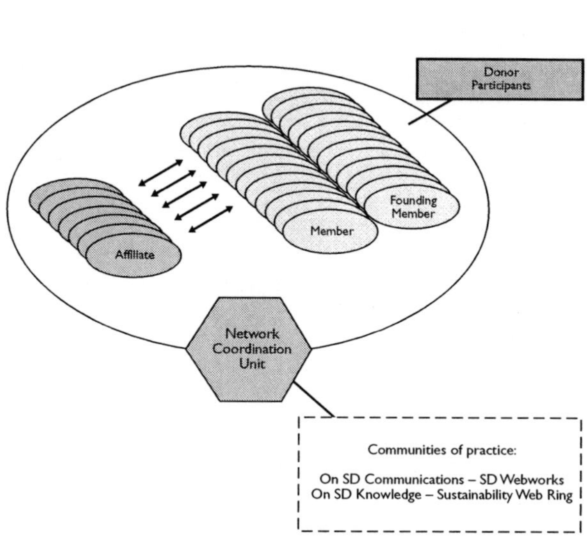

Lesson from these models

The TKN and SDCN each began with a "hub and spokes" approach, with IISD engaged more with individual institutions on a bilateral basis rather than with fostering the network as a whole. We realized that more collaborative models support sharing and creation of new knowledge, better linkages to policy processes and extended relationships, and improved capacity development across the network. We call this the "network advantage," and explore it in more detail in the next section.

Table 3. Summary, forming relationships.

Action	Comments
Allocate time to seek out appropriate partners and begin to build relationships.	Networks fail or under perform because relationships are not built in advance. It is better to have a small number of dedicated working partners rather than dozens of marginally committed partners.
Explore common interests that will hold the network together in the longer term.	Expectations for the network should be driven by whether the organizations are a good fit with each other and support a common agenda, not by the dividing up of financial resources raised for the network.
Learn how prospective partner organizations work.	Build foundation of trust based on realistic expectations of partner performance in the network; mitigate transaction costs of co-managing projects.
Look at research and communications capacity in prospective partners.	All partners need to contribute capacity to share network findings through their own spheres of influence in order to lever engagement strategies.
Develop and apply criteria for membership.	Justification for the invitation of each member to the network, and transparency to those not invited; awareness of strengths and limitations can mitigate obstacles to performance.
Extend relationships beyond core membership.	Keep donors actively informed; donors may wish to learn by doing; networks should not work in a vacuum; innovation can come from others outside of immediate membership; engage target audiences in work of the network.
Move relationships beyond "hub and spokes" approach	More collaborative models support sharing and creation of new knowledge, better linkages to policy processes, improved capacity development across the network.

Organizing relationships

Setting goals and objectives: the network advantage

> *The identification of a concrete, widely shared problem or goal is... generally highlighted as one of the key pillars supporting networks. Networks that fail to develop such a focus do not survive their infant years...*[47]

As we stated in the basic operating principles for formal knowledge networks, these are working networks. The network as a whole needs to have a shared understanding and ownership of goals and objectives, over and above those stated in specific project proposals. It needs a shared plan of action to achieve those goals. Members need to focus on realizing the "network advantage": joint value creation by all the members within the network (aggregating and creating new knowledge); linking that knowledge to policy processes and action, and capacity development across the network.

Too often, a network is designed by a single institution at the project proposal stage in order to obtain the funding to get the network off the ground. The risk with this approach is that the goals and objectives in the funding agreement may not correspond to the expectations of those who eventually join the network. Also, while the proposal documents might describe how members benefit from their participation in the network (financial resources, capacity development and so forth), the documents might not necessarily stimulate them to consider what they can contribute to the benefit of others in the network. And finally, the project documents tend to establish the lead grant recipient as the dominant partner in the network.

Once the membership is in place, each member should review the project proposal documents. They should then consider their own views for the vision, mission and objectives of the network as a whole. Objectives for their participation should include what they hope to contribute to the network (to other members and to the network as a whole). Members should then meet (either face to face or electronically) to come to consensus on the strategic intent of the network. The creation of shared vision, mission and objectives can also form the foundation for the evaluation process for the network. This process is described in the final chapter of this book.

Objectives will shift and change over time. For this reason, Klijn recommends that objectives not be nailed down at the beginning of the network.[48] Our view is that objectives and strategic work plans are necessary and must be written down, but they should be revisited regularly by all members, and amended when appropriate.

Within the goals and objectives for a network, special attention should be paid to the following elements, to reinforce the network advantage:

- links to policy processes and action;
- joint value creation; and
- capacity development.

Links to policy processes and action

The goals, objectives and work plans of formal knowledge networks should clearly articulate the link to the policy process. It is important to remember that the ultimate purpose of a knowledge network is to foster change in specific policies and practices to support sustainable development. This is the foundation of the strategic intention of the network. Therefore those changes desired should be stated up front. The priority areas for work should be selected because a clear outlet for the work can be identified, and not on the basis of the personal interest of an individual researcher alone.

Identifying the link to a given policy process is a precursor to developing the engagement strategy for the network. It is not enough to know which types of decision-makers the network wishes to influence. The network needs to determine whether there are pivotal policy and implementation processes in which decision-makers are involved, and might benefit from the network's research and recommendations. These might include the ongoing negotiations of an international convention or trade agreement; hearings of an international commission; domestic public consultations on a package of legislative instruments; or the development of voluntary or legislative initiatives affecting industry.

While the International Development Research Centre's (IDRC's) PAN (Pan-Asia Networking) program functions in part as an information network, it has incorporated the link to policy processes into its overall agenda. PAN includes in its membership selected decision-makers in the region responsible for the development and implementation of policies on information and communications technologies. PAN's work plans are designed in part to impact and influence these decision-makers in order to improve access to Internet technologies and development information in the region.

Joint value creation

An underlying assumption of networking is that the whole can be greater than the sum of the parts. If the network serves only as an umbrella for a collection of individual projects, it is not realizing its added value potential: to develop new insights through the interaction of different perspectives and approaches. Objectives should explicitly recognize the opportunity for joint value creation by two or more members of the network. Work plans should identify joint projects in addition to individual member projects. If joint projects are not feasible, then mechanisms should be in place for members to review and advise on the work of others.

At the conclusion of the first phase of the Trade Knowledge Network, members acknowledged that the country studies and workshops held by individual members went well, but that the opportunity to exchange experience and work with other members did not really present itself. The network functioned more as a mechanism to fund and manage six trade research projects in Africa, Asia and Latin America. This is being addressed in the second phase. Members will participate in a peer review process for individual country research proposals, and later for the research findings. In addition to country studies and workshops, members are also working on a series of papers on international issues of relevance to more than one member (such as WTO accession and investment regimes).

Capacity development

Knowledge networks require that all members "acquire networking skills, new research management skills, negotiation skills, effective communications skills and, most of all, leadership skills."[49] This is not a North-South transfer of skills and technology issue: rather, it is a recognition that all participants in a network, no matter where they are from, can contribute to and learn from the others in the network. Again, we recommend that this be articulated in the goals and objectives of the network.

In the Trade Knowledge Network, individual members increase their knowledge through case study research. Participants can review one another's work. There is a regular flow of research-related information from members to the group as a whole—or to specific members—depending on the topics and the members' respective interests. Through this research and interaction, the capacity is being built within each member to become a credible and informed voice on the issues in each country. Through the network, each

Southern member brings back the results of its work to a Northern audience starved for empirical Southern work. The realities of trade and sustainable development in the South are poorly understood or ignored by most Northern analysts. The TKN is a mechanism for the Northern members and broader audiences to increase their capacity for understanding the issues.

Developing work plans

A research and communications agenda should be established to guide the work of the organizations in the network. We have observed in some networks the tendency to keep the work plans at the individual project level tied to disbursement of network funds for the execution of those projects. This tends to happen:

a) when a network is driven by an initial grant and a dominant partner (the primary grant recipient) that distributes portions of the grant to members for specific activities; and

b) when members seek and secure additional grants for specific projects under the umbrella of the network.

While the individual projects may be highly successful, they may not serve to drive forward the broader strategic intent of the network. A work plan for the network as a whole is also needed, once again to ensure that the network achieves more than the execution of individual activities. The network plan would at the very least aggregate the individual project plans, in order to monitor timelines, budgets, deliverables and the implementation of communications strategies for each project. But the network plan would also encompass the bigger picture: the checkpoints for reviewing progress on strategic intent and the stages for building relationships with decision-makers. This work plan should be agreed to and monitored by the network as a whole.

Some have suggested that work plans mitigate against other benefits of more informal networking and information sharing; in other words, that structure interferes with spontaneity. What we have observed however is that without work plans, members tend to put their own daily institutional priorities ahead of their network obligations. Without a plan to work together, members tend not to participate in informal interaction either. A work plan serves as a reminder of their commitment to network activities.

Ensuring that members actually execute their portion of the work plan is another challenge in managing relationships. The United Nations Conference on Trade and Development (UNCTAD) notes that "to a large extent, this widespread phenomena of members withdrawing early or not fulfilling their promises can be curbed by securing their commitment to specific, concrete activities, whether it is in the form of an informal verbal agreement [voluntary binding], or a more formal covenant or contract."[50]

Operational support

Creation and role of the secretariat:

Every formal knowledge network needs to decide how the network will be managed. There is only one caveat:

> *Those who would presume to manage a network must first understand that it is seldom they, the managers, who will develop the solution to the problem that the network was formed to address. More often it is the stakeholders themselves who find the answers.*[51]

Network managers should focus on the everyday operations of the network so that the stakeholders are supported in their work. Everyday operations of the network include project management, implementation of the communications and engagement strategies, facilitation of communications among members (including infrastructure development among members where necessary), management of human and financial resources, and evaluation and reporting to funders.

A key question is whether responsibility for those tasks should be centralized with one institution, or shared among several members. In large part, it depends on how the money flows. Usually, if there is a large grant administered by one organization for network activities, then the co-ordination of network operations tends to fall to that organization, which establishes a secretariat or network coordination unit. The challenge with a central secretariat or network coordination unit is to keep the lines of communication open among members so that the institution with the funds does not dominate the network. One solution is to have an umbrella governance agreement which reinforces the ownership of the network and network decision-making among all members. And we highly recommend, should a network manager be put in place, that another individual from the organization administering the grant be nominated to represent that organization in the network. The network manager is responsible equally to all members in the network; the network representative is a stakeholder, responsible for the participation of his or her organization in the research agenda for the network.

The critical role of the network manager

As networks grow and evolve, operations do tend to become more decentralized. Members are more prepared to raise project funds under the umbrella of the network; and members may be more prepared to co-manage projects, including the disbursement of funds to other members, thereby alleviating some of the administrative burden from a co-ordination unit. However, this devolution of responsibilities across network members has its own challenges. Once again, lines of communication need to be kept open to ensure that the network advantage (links to policy processes, joint value creation and capacity development) is not lost in the jumble of individual project activities.

The answer to challenges in centralization and decentralization lies in the role of the network manager (also called a network co-coordinator). As English has stated, "the success of the network depends more than anything else on this individual."[52] Strategic alliance literature often comments on the pivotal role of the "alliance manager"—the individual within the alliance responsible for monitoring the health of the alliance and the compliance of all parties to the alliance agreements. Reinicke, Witte and others agree that the "ability of networks to innovate and produce sustainable results depends on the talent of network managers to keep the ties between actors loose but still close enough to be manageable."[53] The role of the network manager is to:

- manage the flow of information across the network;
- keep the participants engaged;
- balance consultation with members with pushing forward the delivery on network work plans; and
- monitor the financial health of the network.

If resources do not extend to the recruitment of a full- or part-time manager for the network, it might be helpful to prepare a terms of reference for the role, and then establish a management team among network members to ensure the various functions are assigned to individuals.

Communications infrastructure issues

All members should have equal access to network information and the tools to participate effectively. (Chapter 5 addresses internal communications issues in greater depth.) In the early stages of network development, technology assessments should be undertaken for all members and infrastructure development funded and implemented for those who may not have the same ready access to e-mail and the Web. Consideration should also be given to the publishing and outreach capacities of each member. Will the members be able to assist with the communications and engagement strategies for the network, or will additional support be required to strengthen communications services within one or more members?

Human resource issues

Mobility of staff

People move. Technical staff move to the private sector; young professionals go back to school; researchers move to government positions or to other research institutions; government participants may be reassigned to other duties when governments change. Networks need to be designed to accommodate the transitioning in and out of staff. Securing organizational commitment in addition to individual commitment to participate in a network is one step: if a network participant moves on, the organization is obliged to provide another representative to the network, or to withdraw if they have no one else who can take an active role. Network participants should be reminded to keep their organizations up to date on the activities of the network and on the benefits arising from participation so that in the event of change, the organization continues its commitment. A good shared network memory (project documents, records of in person and electronic meetings, work plans) and ongoing evaluation processes can help new representatives to quickly adopt the shared goals and objectives of the network and to become active participants. Nevertheless, there is always a problem with continuity when a key network participant moves on. Good network management can only serve to mitigate, rather than avoid, the impact of such changes.

Role of young professionals in knowledge networks

One of the key components of sustainable development is a conscious consideration of the needs of future generations. Young people will ultimately bear the responsibility for implementing the policies and programs necessary for sustainable development. It is essential that we begin to incorporate their skills, knowledge and ideas into current strategies, as well as develop their capacity to become leaders in the years ahead.

We believe that the formal knowledge network is one of the best tools we have to engage young professionals While previous studies of such networks have duly noted the importance of young researchers and communications staff, they have not investigated either the significance of their contributions to networks, or the means to engage and support them more effectively in network operations. In 2000, we conducted a study of the role of young professionals in networks, to determine what their contributions were to networks, what benefits they derived from their participation and what could be done to strengthen their involvement. Our summary findings from our working paper "Hidden assets: the role of young professionals in knowledge networks"[54] are as follows.

We learned that networks benefit from the inclusion of young professionals in three ways:

1. supporting, strengthening and ensuring the continuity of the research;
2. strengthening internal network processes and interactions; and
3. strengthening the use of communications technologies within the network.

The gains to the young professionals themselves are also significant. We believe that knowledge networks not only support the generation and sharing of knowledge, but they accelerate the professional development of young people, strengthening their ability to contribute to sustainability solutions. Benefits to young professionals include:

- building project management and leadership skills;
- improving access to funds for sustainable development research;
- strengthening their own ICT skills; and
- broadening perspectives on sustainable development.

We observed that there were a number of significant obstacles to the participation of young professionals in networks. These can be overcome by implementing a set of recommendations, including (among others):

- improve the internal communications of the network;
- revise the structure and operations of the network to strengthen the participation of young professionals;
- negotiate "youth friendly" budgets and timelines with funders;
- be proactive in building the decision-making capacity of the young professionals; and
- design networks and associated research projects that will be relevant to young people and future generations.

Gender considerations

The United Nations Educational, Scientific and Cultural Organization (UNESCO) has identified what we also see to be a significant challenge: "How can we enable women to take advantage of the fact that the new management style of the information age relies on traditionally female skills: team work, service orientation and communication skills?"[55] In IISD's formal networks, the percentage of women representing their organizations in a network, actively involved in decision-making, project development and implementation, ranges from 20 to 40 per cent. We would of course like to see the level of participation increase over time. This is an area requiring further investigation, similar to our work on the role of young professionals. There are several current opportunities and challenges that affect the mainstreaming of women in network activities;

- Strengthening communications roles in networks. Strengthening internal communications should serve to improve the interaction of all participants—including women—in the work of the network. Good facilitation by the network manager is necessary to ensure that everyone is engaged and heard in network meetings, electronic conferences, and research and proposal review processes. Utilizing the traditional strengths of women (as noted by UNESCO above) may serve to improve external communications and engagement strategies for the network.
- As stated earlier, the current proliferation of networks is due in part to the electronic technologies which make possible the interaction of members across distance and time. But the use of ICTs can be either an advantage for women or a barrier to their participation, depending upon the region. In Central and Eastern Europe and Southeast Asia, interest in electronic communications tended up to now to be male-dominated because such services evolved from the information technology sector. In Latin America, women are much more actively involved in electronic communications because, in part, Web support services evolved from the library and information field and secretarial services (word and data processing).[56] In Africa, Web services are emerging through alternative media outlets with gender support programs (APC networks, Panos and EcoNews Africa, for example).

Financial resources

Network literature often remarks that the basic structure of networks is consistently underfunded, and often jeopardized as networks mature and donors reduce levels of commitment accordingly. Network operating costs should not be underestimated when developing the initial network grant proposals and subsequent project proposals. There is a good discussion of the financial sustainability of North–South research networks in UNCTAD's 1999 paper, "Making North–South Research Networks Work."[57] The author reviews a range of options for financial resources, including private sector support and revenue generation through membership fees and sales of services.

Some networks—for example, the Global Knowledge Partnership—have instituted membership dues to raise revenues to support the internal operations of the network (internal and external communications, meetings, management of collaborative work tools). This approach requires a critical mass of institutions with resources from which to pay the membership dues, in order to raise sufficient revenue to cover the operating costs. The transactional costs of soliciting the dues can be quite high. Furthermore, most not-for-profit organizations, particularly in the South, do not have access to funds sufficient to cover membership dues on a regular basis.

In the end, UNCTAD observes that longer-term commitments are needed from donor agencies, in particular to "help the research network to continue activities that will never become self-sufficient (such as advocacy work including independent policy research and analysis; special support activities for members in the South)."[58]

In raising revenues for the network, it is therefore extremely important that the network advantage is argued effectively, and that the coordination function is seen to be more than administrative overhead. Members themselves may need to be reminded of this, if they are raising funds for specific projects under the umbrella of the network. However, the network as a whole should discuss and agree to a formula for flowing revenues to the coordination function from specific project grants. The agreement to do so is a measure of the success with which the network has succeeded in becoming more than the sum of its parts.

The allocation of funds, once raised, can be potentially contentious, if the relationships among the members have not been well formed, and if agreements for the division of resources have not been reached in an open and transparent fashion. A representative of one Canadian network, the Atlantic Cooperative Wildlife Ecology Research Network (ACWERN), believes that highly centralized networks, where one agency gets the major grant, results in the other participants getting "the short end of the stick." The distribution of resources is unequal, and works against the spirit and practical research efforts of the network.[59] It takes time and effort to prevent this from happening.

In the first phase of the SDCN, funds for four developing/transitional country partners were divided equally among the organizations that agreed to participate. The four signed virtually identical contracts with IISD for use of the funds. While this was a highly efficient way to proceed, it had two major flaws:

- the accountability of members for performance on their projects was only to IISD, as the provider of funds, and not to each other as network collaborators; and

- the actual needs of the members for funding varied widely. As a result, there was no synergy (no joint value creation) among the member activities. The network value added took place at the top end of the network, by the coordination unit, rather than at the membership level.

In the second phase, the members met in person to review the budget lines in the grants received for the second round of activities. Rather than divide the pot equally, as IISD did in Phase 1, the members themselves did a scan of complementary research activities across their organizations, discussed which merited support for joint communications on those activities and allocated different levels of funding according to the needs expressed by the members. Several members took the lead on individual projects, disbursing funds and monitoring work plans. Interactions among members increased significantly; and the quality of joint projects improved considerably as a result. However, the management of contracts across the network became much more onerous. The challenge in a third phase of SDCN activities will be to reduce the transactional costs of financing and executing collaborative work.

It has been the experience of the CCKN that the network context is a useful way to leverage funds for specific projects. In the first phase of the CCKN, the network grant covered network operations (meetings, coordination and communications) and seed funding for proposal development. Members then sourced funds from other donors for specific projects which had been reviewed and approved by the network as a whole. This approach has transferred some of the challenges of revenue generation to the members, which strengthens the sense of ownership among members and reduces reducing some of the financial and management pressures on the coordination unit.

Table 4. Summary, organizing relationships.

Action	Comments
Reconcile funding proposal/grant agreement with partner objectives.	Leads to shared ownership; partners should focus on what they can contribute as well as gain; downplays lead organization (grant recipient) as the dominant partner; lays the foundation for evaluation.

Action	Comments
Focus on the network advantage in developing goals, objectives, work plans.	
Link to policy processes.	Purpose of a knowledge network is to foster change in specific policies and practices; priority areas for work should be selected because a clear outlet for the work can be identified.
Identify opportunities for joint value creation in the work plan.	Develop new insights through the interaction of different perspectives and approaches.
Include process for capacity development in the objectives.	Recognize that all participants in a network, no matter where they are from, can contribute to and learn from the others in the network.
Set in place a master work plan for the whole network	Ensures that the network achieves more than the execution of individual member activities; reinforces the importance of network obligations as part of, rather than in competition with, day-to-day institutional priorities.
Decide how the network will be managed	
Role of Secretariat (consider centralized and decentralized operating modes).	Support the stakeholders in their work.
Role of manager.	Monitors the health of the network and the compliance of partners to their obligations; keeps the lines of communication open.
Review technical infrastructure and communications capacity of members.	All members should have equal access to network information and the tools to participate effectively; members need to assist with the communications and engagement strategies.
Human resources	
Mobility: Design networks to accommodate the transitioning in and out of staff.	People move. Good network management can only serve to mitigate, rather than avoid, the impact of such changes.

Action	Comments
Young professionals: Recognize and capitalize on their pivotal role in supporting and strengthening networks.	Build the capacity of the next generation of decision-makers; strengthen the substantive research and the internal and external communications processes of the network.
Take gender considerations into account: reinforce the communications roles.	Utilizing the traditional skills of women (team work, service orientation and communications skills) will strengthen the network.
Explore options for financial resources, raising revenues; in particular to support the coordination/network management functions.	Basic structure of networks is consistently underfunded, and often jeopardized as networks mature and donors reduce levels of commitment accordingly.

Formalizing relationships: Network governance

The importance of governance structures is often underestimated.[60]

Network governance is not network management. Network management addresses day-to-day activities, such as planning, handling of staff and financial resources, monitoring work plans and so forth. Governance is the formalization of the relationships among the members. A governance structure is rarely put in place at the beginning of a network. Form follows function: in networks, it may take some time for network members to work through how a network will operate, what its goals and objectives should be, and how to achieve those most effectively. In the process of operationalizing the network, the governance arrangements will become more clear, and can be codified in a governance agreement.

It may be wise to wait a year or more before formalizing governance, particularly in larger networks. In the interim, the funding agreements from donors may provide a sufficient framework for accountability. If governance discussions are undertaken too early in the life of the network, there is the risk that the strongest or most vocal members will dictate the governance arrangements without a clear picture of how the network will really function over several years. While establishing the governance structure is of strategic importance, it does not necessarily take a great deal of time to configure if much of the work has already been done in forming and managing the relationships within the network.

Vision, mission and principles

Governance begins with finalizing agreement among all members on the vision, mission, goals and objectives of the network (what is the network all about). Governance also includes the articulation of network principles ("partnership principles" or "operating principles")—the fundamental or underlying values of the members that determine how they participate in the network in order to achieve the mission of the network. These principles become the values of the network as a whole. (Chapter 2 provides a starting point for a network discussion on principles.)

The Global Development Network developed a set of five principles for informing its governance structure:[61]

1. Independence – quality or state of being independent; self governing;
2. Openness – completely free from concealment; exposed to general view or knowledge;
3. Effectiveness – producing a decided, decisive or desired effect;
4. Democracy – measures to include representativeness and broad participation; and
5. Plurality – encompassing a diversity of disciplines and paradigms.

With the vision and values recorded in the governance agreement, the network provides its members with a consistent reference point agreed to by all if they appear to be drifting off mission.

Roles of members, decision-making parameters

Governance sets down the membership arrangements (who is part of the network) and the duties and responsibilities of members (what in general the members are expected to do). The governance structure makes clear the decision-making process: what types of decisions does the membership have the authority to make, or to delegate their representatives to make:

- On what issues does the network require consensus (e.g., changes in strategic intent)?
- On what issues does the network require a simple majority, or 2/3 majority vote (e.g., admission of new members; review and acceptance of project proposals)?

- On what issues does the network require only the input of the membership to other members or the secretariat serving the network? (e.g., review of research findings)?

Depending on the size of the network, the decisions are made either by the membership as a whole, or by representatives nominated to a decision-making body (a board or council).

The Sustainable Development Communications Network determined that certain decisions should be taken only by the founding members, acting as an Executive Council for the Network. Other decisions could be taken by the Members. The following decision matrix is part of the governance agreement.[62]

Table 5. The decision matrix.

Issue	Who can vote	Process		
		Consensus	Vote	Input
Establishing vision of the network	Founding Members	X		
Amendments to the Network Agreement	Founding Members	X		
Selecting new Members	Founding Members		X	
Selecting new Affiliate Members	Members			X
Developing specific projects	Members			X
Pursuing funding for network and specific projects	Members			X

Consensus – Members must reach agreement before a decision is taken.

Vote – The decision will be made based on 2/3-majority vote

Input – Where one full member has primary decision-making responsibility in respect of a matter delegated to it by members, it must solicit input from all members prior to acting. Other members are expected to adopt a proactive response on the issue. Received input will be considered when making the decision. If input is not received within a reasonable time, it will be assumed that the member does not wish to provide input on the issue.

Network structure

The more recent literature on alliances and networks reflects a shift away from more rigorous legal agreements, in part because networks change and evolve. As functions change, so too will the form of the network:

> *The best governance approaches are tailor-made to fit each alliance, but they still share at least one common theme: the traditional, paternalistic definition of governance—the CEO and the board—is obsolete. Today's alliances are better governed through several layers of decision-makers.*[63]

However, some formally defined understanding of the structure of the network is still important. In the section on forming relationships, we presented several examples of the sphere of relationships that can be formed and fostered within a knowledge network. In the section below, we describe three different network structures in order to compare the mechanics of decision-making, roles of members and the lead organization(s), options for various committees, and governance documentation.

Strategic alliance

Strategic alliances in the private sector are "long-term purposeful arrangements among distinct but related organizations that allow those firms to gain or sustain competitive advantage vis à vis their competitors outside the network."[64] Alliances are formed to improve the business position of each of the individual firms in the alliance. In the civil society sector, each partner must ask itself how a proposed alliance will further its competitive advantage and strengthen its position in the marketplace of ideas. Alliances can either be built around a shared goal or to further the individual goals of the respective partners. An alliance results in real value appropriation from one partner to another across the alliance. Whether the partners have a shared goal or enter the alliance in order to improve their own performance, the driving force is survival: the need for size and speed against the competition. Strategic alliances with clearly stated objectives to acquire skills and know-how from each partner are more successful. Partners do not necessarily need to have equal status in the relationship; alliances can function with a dominant partner or partners.

A formal knowledge network structure might adapt the following elements from the strategic alliance approach:

- The decision-making structure would be grouped around functions within the network's "value chain." That value chain might include members involved in research activities; members specializing in participatory processes and communications; and the donors group acting as investors in the network. Depending on the size of the network, each group might have its own committee to monitor work plans.

- An assurance group for the alliance might be established with experts outside of the alliance membership.
- An alliance oversight council might include one representative from each alliance committee plus the assurance group. If the alliance has a limited number of members then the council might include all members.
- The lead organization would retain the role of alliance manager.
- Documentation: Depending on the size of the network, each group might negotiate its own agreement with the alliance manager detailing obligations and levels of decision-making. If the alliance has a limited number of members, then it might be sufficient to have one alliance agreement for all parties to sign.

Research network model

This is the approach most frequently taken by not–for-profit organizations. Members tend to view themselves as equal partners in the relationship.

- Members (core membership) consist of the change agents within the network: those organizations that will be doing the work of the network. By focusing on them as the heart of the network, it becomes much easier to put evaluation mechanisms in place that focus on development outcomes (changes in actions, approaches and behaviours).
- Depending on the size of the network, core members might act as a governing council of the whole, or they might elect representatives to the governing council or executive committee.
- In keeping with the engagement strategies of the network, members might choose to appoint representatives of their target audiences to the governing council.
- Other categories of members (donors, observers) might form separate advisory committees, which would give advice to the governing council.
- The lead organization(s) establishes the secretariat as services provider to the network. The secretariat has decision-making authority over the services it provides. The lead organization

then becomes a member within the appropriate category of membership defined by the network.

- The secretariat could be moved from one member to another.
- Documentation: Usually in this model, there is only one governance agreement—or a Memorandum of Understanding or Statement of Principles—to be signed by all members.

Autonomous legal entity

At some stage in the evolution of a network, members may wish to establish the network as an autonomous legal entity, separating the network completely from the original founding organization(s). The new entity would be formally incorporated in a jurisdiction chosen by the members. The new entity would become the legal proprietor of the network's brand name, intellectual and financial assets, and liabilities. The staff of the new entity would be responsible for network management. A CEO would be appointed, reporting to a board of directors. The board would be composed of representatives of network members. There may be several reasons for taking this approach:

- Members wish to reduce the influence of the founding organization(s) in the network.
- Members believe that the sourcing and distribution of grants to support the network's activities may be handled more effectively through an independent entity. Donors may not, for some reason, be willing or able to fund the lead institution, and individual members might not have the interest or capacity to seek and manage funds from donors for network activities. Consequently a new institution may be required to manage the financing of the network. Also, the independent entity may reduce the potential conflicts of interest which exist when the member institutions themselves source grants under the umbrella of the network for network activities, but then apply those resources for their own institutional objectives.
- Members wish to approportion the risk and successes involved in operating the network across the membership, rather than allowing the lead organization(s) to assume the risk and success.

We are cautious about this model. Our view is that setting in place a new organizational structure in many ways defeats the purpose of networks and alliances. The approach centralizes rather than distributes responsibilities. Members are connected to the organization rather than to each other. The network advantage—links to policy processes, joint value creation and capacity development—is diminished as the network looks inward rather than toward those it wishes to engage and change.

Additional issues to be addressed in formalizing governance

Not all of the issues noted below will be relevant to all networks, but they should be considered in developing a governance agreement.

Table 6. Governance issues.

Issue	Comments
Approval of network project proposals and results.	How does the network approve a project proposal brought forward by a member? Once the project is complete, does the network review and approve the results of the project before it can be published or released? Under what circumstances would a network not approve a member's work?
Roles for special interest committees, task forces and advisory groups.	Again, this is contingent on the size and complexity of the network. A larger network may wish to establish a committee to monitor, for example, the inclusion of young professionals or women in the work of the networks. Usually, it is sufficient in the governance agreement to make provision for the establishment of ad hoc committees, the terms of reference for which can be established by the membership at some later date.
Documenting the functions of the secretariat.	In addition to the roles and responsibilities of members, the role of the secretariat should also be described.
Procedures for withdrawing from the network.	The governance agreement should require certain terms and conditions to be met before a member can withdraw. Usually, if the member has received funding for executing a network project, withdrawal from the network may only occur upon conclusion of their obligations as set out in their contracts with their funders. Provision should be made for members who do not have any contractual obligations related to network projects to withdraw from the network at any time by giving a notification of intent of a specific time period prior to withdrawing (for example, 30 days).

Issue	Comments
Dispute resolution.	UNCTAD recommends that formal procedures be established within a network "to deal with situations in which no consensus on important (policy) issues can be achieved within the governance structure. Without such mechanisms, research networks will be unable to take strong, consistent positions on important issues, and they will be ineffective in situations that require energetic leadership."[65]
Clarity on intellectual property rights.	Unless the network is a separate legal entity, the governance agreement may be silent on this. The assumption is that the assignment of intellectual property rights is determined in the funding agreements for specific projects and activities undertaken by members. However, it may be important to include in the governance agreement a clause that requires members to acknowledge in publications, software or other products and processes that the intellectual property was developed under the auspices of the network.
Clarity on assets and liabilities.	Again, unless the network is a separate legal entity, the governance agreement may be silent on this.
Limitations on advocacy positions and other public statements.	Members may wish to consider whether and how the network can speak on behalf of the members, and whether there needs some clarity on how to represent positions of the network which may not be the positions of individual member organizations.
Clarity on who has the authority in member organizations or the lead organization to make decisions related to the network	Experts in strategic alliance and relationships planning warn against falling into the trap of setting up shadow governance, "when those managing the alliance must defer all real decisions to other parts of the company."[66]

Lifespan of a formal knowledge network: closure and renewal

Members are often loath to terminate a network, even when it has outlived its purpose or is no longer functional. But often a network is established without a clear view of what the lifespan of the network should be. Our experience shows that networks may take up to five years to become established, produce concrete work, and begin to have real influence through their engagement strategies. The most productive period for a network may be the five to 10 years after it was launched. Too often, we see networks planned for the short term, around funding agreements, but with an underlying assumption that the network will exist in perpetuity once established.

We strongly recommend that network designers estimate the lifespan of the network in the planning stages, and that checkpoints be built into the structure to either renew or wind down the activities of the network. The governance structure should be established for a set period of time (three years, for example), with a sunset clause or a pre-set period of evaluation incorporated into the governance agreement. In the final year of the agreement, the governance structure should be evaluated, and decisions taken about whether to wind up the network, or amend or transform the structure. A sunset clause in the agreement provides a graceful means for members to not renew their participation rather than activate notice for withdrawal from the network. It also provides the opportunity to renew the vision of network.[67]

Table 7. Summary, formalizing relationships.

Action	Comments
Governance should be discussed after members have worked together for a period of time, organizing their activities and their relationships with each other.	Members need to work through goals, objectives, work plans, responsibilities and so forth. Governance codifies these parameters rather than dictates them in advance. If governance agreements are prepared too early in the process, they will require significantly more revision throughout the lifespan of the network.
Begin with finalizing agreement on goals, objectives; articulate network principles.	Records what the network is all about and the underlying values of the members in the governance agreement. Provides the reference point if the network appears to be drifting off mission.
Codify the membership arrangements (who is part of the network).	See section 1 on forming relationships.
Set the decision-making parameters.	Makes clear what requires consensus by the network as a whole, majority vote or merely input to other members or the secretariat.

Action	Comments
Customize and finalize the network structure.	Describes the mechanics of decision-making, roles of members and the lead organization(s), options for various committees, and governance documentation.
Scope out and resolve additional governance issues and record in governance agreement.	See table on additional issues above.
Agree to the lifespan of the network. Include a sunset clause or pre-set period of evaluation in the governance agreement.	Provides a graceful means for members to not renew their participation; provides the opportunity to renew the vision of the network.

Institutionalizing relationships: Managing organizational change in response to network participation

In the private sector literature on strategic alliances and business networks, writers have observed a natural progression from corporate, hierarchical structures, to more decentralized, collaborative approaches within companies, and finally to networks and alliances. Networks and alliances are more successful if the individual members have begun to move toward collaborative approaches within their own organizations.

> *Collaborative individualism and the emergence of strategic networks go hand in hand. They are part of the same mindset—part of the reaction against hierarchies, the focus on individual competence, and the search for collaboration.*[68]

Within an organization, collaborative individualism requires that the organization constantly keeps its mission at the forefront, in order to maintain the individual commitment to achieving the mission. This becomes even more critical when forming alliances and networks: the mission of the network or alliance has to be complementary with the mission of the member organization. Without this internal alignment of the member organization with the network, one begins to run into mixed loyalties and goal ambiguity, both of which will eventually undermine the network.

We have observed that this trend to move from hierarchical structures towards the networked organization is taking place more slowly within civil society organizations. There still appears to be a separation between institutions, with their internal management structures, and networks that have identities of their own—rather than organizations internalizing and capitalizing on their participation in networks.

Some part of this is due to the chronic under-resourcing of most civil society organizations. This leads to short attention spans for activities like networks, unless the work is well integrated into the organizational priorities. When an organization is invited or seeks to join a network, it should consider in advance what impact the network might have on the organization itself. The introduction of external partners, with their own viewpoints and management processes, inevitably clashes with existing corporate cultures. Institutional priorities may well clash with network priorities unless they are proactively aligned.

Participation in the network has the potential to transform the member organizations by introducing new work processes, ideas and values. Recognition that there will be these impacts, and that there will be a transition period as an organization becomes attuned to network processes, will serve to mitigate transaction costs.

Assessing the performance of individuals within networks is another area requiring some thought. Usually, people working in a network are evaluated by their institutions with respect to their performance against institutional objectives rather than network objectives. If institutional priorities are clashing with network priorities, it is unlikely that the individual participant will receive the support and recognition for his or her contribution to a network, even though that contribution may be significant, valued by other participants in the network and funded. Even more problematic is the situation where a participant is not meeting his or her network commitments. If the network is not seen to be integral to the objectives of the member institution, it is more difficult for other members and the network manager to persuade the individual to meet timelines and produce deliverables.

Finally, an organization should look carefully at all the networks and alliances and partnerships to which it is committed. We would recommend that organizations annually review all of their relationships in networks, alliances and partnerships, and consider which ones are performing well, which relationships need strengthening and which have run their course and should be concluded.

> *A few solid high performing alliances would be easier to manage and grow than hundreds of non-performing partnerships.*[69]

Table 8. Summary, institutionalizing relationships.

Action	Comments
Ensure that institutional mission and network mission are complementary.	Avoid goal ambiguity, mixed loyalties of staff working for organization as well as network.
Integrate network priorities into institutional priorities.	Reduce or avoid conflicting priorities and mixed loyalties of staff.
Be open to change processes that come with collaboration.	Mitigate transaction costs. Networking with other organizations has the potential to transform internal work processes, cultures and values.
Staff should be evaluated on their performance/contribution to the networks they are involved with, not just on performance within their institution.	When network and institutional priorities are aligned, staff should be supported and rewarded equally for contribution to networks and to their institution; poor performance within networks should be reviewed and dealt with.
Review all relationships annually; focus on solid, high performing relationships; strengthen relationships where necessary and conclude or withdraw from non-performing relationships.	A few solid relationships are easier to manage and grow.

Endnotes

38 Witte, J.H. *et al. Beyond Multilateralism: Global Public Policy Networks*, International Politics and Society, 2, (2000), <http://www.fes.de/ipg/ipg2_2000/artwitte.html>.

39 Dent, H.S. *Corporation of the Future*, quoted by D. Limerick and B. Cunnington, *Managing the New Organization: A Blueprint for Networks and Strategic Alliances* (San Francisco: Jossey-Bass, 1994), p. 79.

40 Blau, Andrew. *More Than Bit Players: A Report to the Sundra Foundation*, May 2001, p. 16, <http://www.sundra.org/documents/morefinal.pdf>.

41 Kalmbach, C. and C. Roussel. *Dispelling the myths of alliances*, Andersen Consulting, 2000, <http://www.accenture.com>.

42 Lewis, J.D. *Partnerships for Profit: Structuring and Managing Strategic Alliances* (New York: MacMillan, 1990). pp. 225–228.

43 Klijn, E.H. and J.F.M. Koppenjan. "Public management and policy networks," *Public Management*, 2 (2000), p. 141.

44 Gladwell, M. *The Tipping Point: How little things can make a big difference* (Boston: Little, Brown, 2000).

45 Lewis, pp. 284–285.

46 Climate Change Knowledge Network Governance Agreement, <http://www.cckn.net/members.asp>.

47 *Making North-South Research Networks Work*, United Nations Conference on Trade and Development, 2001, <http://www.unctad.org/en/subsites/dite/2_stech/2_icts.htm>.

48 Klijn, pp. 148–149.

49 The Impact Group. "Strengthening Environmental Research in Canada," Discussion Paper (unpublished, 1999), p. 20.

50 *Making North-South Research Networks Work.*

51 Reinicke, W.H. and F. Deng. *Critical Choices: The United Nations, Networks, and the Future of Global Governance* (Ottawa: IDRC, 2000), pp. xv–xvi.

52 English, P. "The Governance of Networks: The experience of IDRC's Social Sciences Division in Subsaharan Africa," *IDRC report* (unpublished, 1995), p. 4.

53 Witte, J.H. *et al.*

54 Cole *et al.*, *Hidden Assets: The Role of young professionals in knowledge networks*, IISD Working Paper (Winnipeg: IISD, 2000), <http://www.iisd.org/pdf/2001/networks_youth_networks.pdf>.

55 *Women on the Net*, UNESCO <http://www.unesco.org/webworld/women/womennet.html>.

56 Interviews with representatives of the Association for Progressive Communications and International Women's Tribune Centre, September, 1995.

57 *Making North-South Research Networks Work.*

58 *Ibid.*

59 Meeting of the Canadian Environmental Sciences Network (March 2001).

60 English, P. *Governance Structures of Networks in Sub-Saharan Africa*, and A. Bernard, *IDRC Networks: an Ethnographic Perspective* (Ottawa: IDRC, 1996), p. 53.

61 *Final Report of the Governance Working Group*, The Global Development Network, 2000, p. 2, <http://www.gdnet.org/pdfs/finalgovreport.pdf>.

62 Sustainable Development Communications Network Governance Agreement, 2001, <http://www.sdcn.org>.

63 *The Science of Alliances: Governance Roles and Responsibilities*, C. Roussel, Accenture, 2001, <http://www.accenture.com>.

64 Jarillo, C.J. *Strategic Networks–Creating the Borderless Organization* (Oxford: Butterworth-Heinemann, 1993).

65 *Making North-South Research Networks Work.*

66 *The Science of Alliances: Picking the right partner*, C. Roussel, Accenture, 2000, <http://www.accenture.com>.

67 Titi, Vangile. *Building Partnerships for Sustainable Development*, Working Paper (IISD, 1993).

68 Limerick and Cunnington, p. 113.

69 Friedman, L.G. *The Elusive Strategic Alliance*, in *Building Strategic Relationships* (San Francisco: Jossey-Bass, 1995), p. 115.

Chapter 5
Helping Knowledge Networks Work

Introduction

At the heart of knowledge networks are people working together. Ideas are generated. Projects are proposed. Activities are implemented. Learnings are documented and shared to spark new ideas and begin the cycle over again. However, these processes do not occur automatically. Network projects can miss deadlines, cause frustrations and undercut the feelings of mutual admiration and appreciation that may have attracted members in the first place.

Joining a knowledge network entails a long-term commitment to collaborative effort. In order for a knowledge network to exist at all, careful attention must be given to how staff from member organizations will interact. This attention must go beyond what tools they will use to communicate. It must also include an appreciation for the varying communications styles of staff in member organizations. It must include the establishment of ground rules for responding to ideas and criticism. It must tackle the difficult issue of managing conflict. Without attention to these details, it is impossible to achieve project objectives and maintain the long-term health of the network.

The skills of forming and working within virtual teams are essential for staff working within sustainable development knowledge networks. Unfortunately, the management styles and systems of most civil society organizations (CSOs) constrain the effectiveness of inter-organizational virtual teamwork. Given the rapid increase in joint projects and collaborations for sustainable development, however, CSOs must begin to examine how they work together across vast geographical and cultural differences. The technical possibility of such collaboration among CSOs has created a necessity to do so in order to remain competitive in attracting continued project funding. The introduction of new information and communication technologies has fundamentally disrupted the work of civil society organizations.[70]

This chapter focuses on the challenges faced by the formal knowledge networks with which the International Institute for Sustainable Development (IISD) works. These networks include the Climate Change Knowledge Network (CCKN),[71] Trade Knowledge Network (TKN),[72] and the Sustainable Development Communications Network (SDCN).[73] These networks are international in membership and rely on virtual teams for the development of collaborative projects and communications activities.

Virtual teams

A virtual team, like every team, is a group of people who interact through interdependent tasks guided by common purpose. Unlike conventional teams, however, virtual teams work across space, time and organizational boundaries with links strengthened by webs of communication technologies.[74] Working across numerous boundaries, however, brings with it challenges to effective and efficient project management.

Duarte and Snyder categorize the complexity of a virtual team according to the number of boundaries that the team crosses:[75]

1. has members from more than one organization;
2. has members from more than one function;
3. has members who transition on and off the team;
4. is geographically dispersed over more than three contiguous time zones;
5. is geographically dispersed so that some team members are 8–12 hours apart;
6. has members from more than two national cultures;
7. has members whose native language is different from the majority of other team members;
8. has members who do not have equal access to electronic communication and collaboration technology.

(1–2 matched characteristics indicates some complexity; 3–5 indicates moderate complexity; and 6–8 indicates high complexity.)

With the exception of the last item that addresses technological matters, the list deals exclusively with cultural issues. Cultural boundaries and conflicts present more challenges in virtual teamwork than technology *per se*. Technology merely helps people cross cultural boundaries more easily and builds expectations that it can and should be done.

Most sustainable development knowledge network teams are highly complex which makes it difficult for these networks to function effectively. In addition, member organizations are development institutions that frequently lack many of the critical success factors for participation in complex virtual teams. Most non-government organizations simply have not invested strongly in results-based human resource policies, training and development, standardized organizational policies, and communication and collaboration technology. For that reason, emerging civil society knowledge networks tend to include primarily elite institutions from around the world. These are organizations with substantial track records in individual project management that are more likely to have attracted the resources necessary for virtual teamwork.

Teams in knowledge networks

Knowledge networks may include two distinct types of virtual teams in their operations: management teams and project teams. In some cases, however, there may be considerable overlap in the individuals serving in each type of team. For example, the senior researchers working on project teams within the Climate Change Knowledge Network (CCKN) are also members of the management team.

The network management team usually includes high-level representation from the member organizations and is tasked with the ongoing evolution of network objectives, strategy, membership and structure. Ideally, the management team meets periodically (one or two times per year) to review its governance and progress on projects as well as to determine what structural issues and thematic projects should be dealt with during the next period. The network management team has relatively stable membership, thus permitting the development of longer-term relationships and trust.

In contrast, project teams can be extremely fluid. Within any particular project, different individuals with appropriate research, communications and project management expertise may represent a member organization at various points in time. As well, each project may involve different member organizations. Project teams may face resource constraints prohibiting the possibility of face-to-face meetings and tend to work almost completely through the use of electronic collaboration spaces.

The level of activity and enthusiasm in these collaboration spaces corresponds directly to the level of ambiguity and innovativeness of the project. According to David Weinberger, editor of the *Journal of the Hyperlinked Organization*, "clearly there are collaborative projects that aim solely at efficient execution of an established plan. Nothing wrong with those! In those project spaces, conversation is only required when something goes wrong. Project management software helps to manage these routinized projects. But the more truly collaborative a project is, the louder and stronger and more animated will be the voices emerging from the project work place."[76]

Examples of project teams from knowledge networks hosted by the International Institute for Sustainable Development (IISD) include:

SDCN project teams

- Rio+5 web site and Webcast – Earth Council and IISD
- EcoLegis Environmental Law Databases – Fundación Ambiente y Recursos Naturales (FARN) and Regional Environmental Centre for Central and Eastern Europe (REC)
- Sustainable Livelihoods Module – Environnement et développement du tiers-monde (ENDA-TM), Development Alternatives (DA), IISD and Stockholm Environment Institute (SEI)
- Sustainable Cities Module – REC, ENDA, FARN and DA
- Water Management Module – DA, ENDA, REC and SEI
- Public Participation Module – FARN, REC and SEI

CCKN project teams

- Climate Change Capacity Project – Africa – ENDA and IISD
- Capacity Building for Latin American and Caribbean Negotiators – The Center for Sustainable Development of the Americas (CSDA) and The Institute for Environmental Studies (IVM)
- "On Behalf of My Delegation...": A Survival Guide for Developing Country Climate Negotiators – CSDA, ENDA, IISD and IVM
- Clean Development Mechanism Project – CSDA and the World Resources Institute (WRI)

To date, the performance record of the virtual teams in these networks has been mixed. While a number of useful products have been created, the process has often been arduous, confusing and stressful. We have learned by doing—a process that has helped us to understand precisely how difficult and costly international collaboration can be.

Civil society organizations may lack experience with working in collaborative international teams. Despite their commitment to participation and inclusiveness, sustainable development organizations have tended to be structured in hierarchical fashions that tend to impede the activities of knowledge network virtual teams. Such teams often work flexibly across traditional institutional structure and boundaries. Nevertheless, we believe that international civil society organizations can begin to develop the processes and procedures necessary to meet the challenges confronting them.

Crossing cultural boundaries

Culture is often defined as a set of learned mores, values, attitudes and meanings that are shared by members of a group. It is one of the primary ways in which one group differentiates itself from another. It affects people's assumptions, behaviours and expectations about leadership practices, work habits and team norms. There are three types of culture that can affect a virtual team: national, organizational and functional. Each team member brings his or her culture and, as the team evolves, the unique blend of team members' national functional, and organizational cultures create a unique team culture.[77]

National cultures

The patterns associated with national culture are often established in childhood and are the most embedded. These, coupled with life experiences, create the differences in behaviour and thinking that exist when we talk about a person's cultural background.[78] In the context of knowledge networks, we must also consider language and seasonality as parts of national culture influencing virtual teams.

General issues

Duarte and Snyder outline six dimensions of national culture.[79] These six dimensions affect how virtual teams communicate and work together:

1. Power distance – Extent to which the less powerful members expect and accept that power is distributed equally.
2. Uncertainty avoidance – Degree of structure required for a task.
3. Individualism-collectivism – Preference to act as individuals rather than as members of groups.
4. Masculinity-femininity – Extent to which a "masculine" orientation—concerned with things such as earnings, possessions and visible success—has priority over a more "feminine" orientation toward nurturing, cooperation and sharing.
5. Long-term-short-term – Degree of focus on parsimony, family orientation, virtuous behaviour, and acquisition of skill and knowledge.
6. High or low context – Amount of sensing and extra information needed to make decisions versus "just the facts."

While most staff in international sustainable development knowledge networks are aware that these differences exist, it can often be difficult to determine the best course through a decision-making process when multiple individuals are involved—each with a different combination of these differences. A balance must be struck between respecting differences of opinion based on national culture and needing to come to a decision on a course of action. A balance must also be struck between understanding that national culture differences exist and allowing people the freedom to not follow stereotypes based on their national origin.

Underestimating the importance of cultural differences may lead to conflicts within the network that require greater personal investments to heal. For example, in 1999 Environnement et développement du tiers-monde (ENDA-TM) in Senegal offered to host the annual meeting of the Sustainable Development Communications Network. Funds for this meeting were available through a project grant received by the Canadian-based International Institute for Sustainable Development (IISD). Having worked together on various projects over the previous three years, the ENDA network representative indicated that his organization would organize all necessary logistics within the budget parameters and seek reimbursement from IISD following the meeting. When the IISD accounting department indicated that this arrangement would require a written contract, the ENDA representative was deeply offended. He felt IISD's request indicated a lack of trust. Most confusing to him was that according to the proposed arrangement, it was ENDA, not IISD that was in the most vulnerable position if funds were not transferred to cover incurred expenses. Culturally, as the host of the meeting, it was important to him to show trust for IISD; the contract seemed antithetical to the spirit of the collaboration. It required significant time to resolve the issue; it took even longer to rebuild the sense of personal camaraderie and trust required to work effectively together on additional projects.

In addition to these general cross-cultural issues, IISD has encountered two additional issues confronting knowledge networks:

1. how to work in multiple first, second and third languages; and
2. when to get the work done, taking into account regional holidays and seasons.

Languages

International knowledge networks will usually involve individuals with several different native languages. Given the international nature of sustainable development, however, many staff working on knowledge network virtual teams may have experience living and working in countries and languages other than the one(s) in which they were born and raised. Staff are frequently multi-lingual with knowledge of local and international languages (e.g., English, French and Spanish). Nevertheless, English has become the common language for knowledge networks within management and project teams. Meeting minutes, project proposals and network products tend to be produced in English. Informal bilateral communications among network members or network members and the secretariat may occur in other languages.

If some team members are less comfortable working in English, longer time schedules should be established for interaction to allow them to read through documents and to respond. Additionally, text-based modes of communication and collaboration should be favoured over teleconferencing. It can be difficult for team members to understand English spoken with a wide variety of accents on the telephone or Internet video. And they may be reluctant to speak if they cannot find the correct words to express their thoughts, especially if other team members are not well known to them. Text-based forms of collaboration permit people to reread their own and other comments. During face-to-face meetings, frequent coffee breaks should be scheduled to provide individuals time to check their understanding of issues with others who speak their native language.

Seasons and holidays

In addition to the obvious difficulties in working across multiple time zones, knowledge networks must contend with the challenges of working across seasons and holidays in multiple cultures and both hemispheres. For example, many offices in Europe and North America are nearly empty during July and August as staff leave for summer vacations. Likewise, institutions in Argentina may be short-staffed from December through January as summer holidays and Christmas combine. Fortunately, the December break also coincides with Christmas, Hanukkah and Ramadan celebrations in other parts of the world. Meanwhile, equatorial countries may concentrate vacations around April or September, the transitions between rainy and dry seasons when the weather is pleasant. In Latin America and the Philippines, the April holidays may also coincide with Easter celebrations. Scheduling of work becomes complex and becomes concentrated within very small windows of opportunity. International knowledge networks seem to concentrate their activities in March-June and again from October-December. The other five months tend to be used for working on projects undertaken by individual organizations or regional partnerships that share the same cultural and seasonal holidays.

Organizational cultures

Within every group—including knowledge networks—there are individuals with divergent values and assumptions that influence its collective behaviour. On the most basic level, there are two sets of polar opposites within which groups can locate themselves:

- Clan versus market – Clan culture views the organization or network as an extended family and its leaders as parent figures. Members are highly committed; teamwork is paramount. Market cultures are results-oriented with competitive members and aggressive leaders.
- Hierarchy versus adhocracy – Hierarchical cultures are formal, governed by procedures with a focus on structure and control. Adhocracy cultures are dynamic and adaptive, with a great deal of risk taking and innovation.

If a knowledge network team is to work together harmoniously, the individuals involved must begin to develop a process of working together across organizational cultures. This team's culture may be different from that of any particular member organization, although it will likely be influenced strongly by the culture of the network manager or lead organization. If there is a mismatch between the team's existing culture and the demands of its task, the team may decide to develop new norms or to add new members who represent the organizational culture it is trying to create.[80]

Planning and prototyping

Some of the most important elements of organizational culture are the norms for developing and implementing new projects. Virtually all new projects and ideas result from duelling approaches: "a wish list" of specifications and the prototypes that attempt to embody them. Often prototypes confirm that what we desire is unrealistic or ill-conceived. Conversely, they can also reveal that our wishes were not imaginative enough.[81] In complex and rapidly evolving fields, it is almost impossible for people to articulate clear specifications for what they want until after they have seen a prototype. Managing the dialogue between specifications and prototypes is essential to innovation in design. The balance between the two is a function of institutional cultures.

In the field of international sustainable development, this balance is played out as a tension over the size and scope of projects undertaken. Specifications are embodied in project proposals, while prototypes often take the form of pilot projects. Specification-oriented organizations will tend to favour projects with extensive preliminary research, and longer time frames for implementation. In order to recoup proposal development costs, the budgets will be larger. Prototype-oriented institutions will have internal processes that favour the development of numerous smaller proposals for pilot projects. These projects will be of shorter duration and provide ample opportunity for revision, expansion or abandonment of an idea. In establishing its knowledge networks and their initial suites of projects, IISD has favoured fast prototyping over extensive research and development of detailed proposals. Each project within a knowledge network builds upon the lessons, experience and momentum of the last. We have found that small projects have built the relationships and capacity necessary to undertake larger expansion projects as the relationships within the network matures.

For example, in 1999 the Sustainable Development Communications Network created a prototype of an online resource kit about non-profit Web management, the SD Webworks <http://sdgateway.net/webworks/>. Funding for the site was sourced as part of a broader network proposal to the Canadian International Development Agency (CIDA). The site contained overviews, recommendations and case studies of good practice in planning, managing and evaluating sustainable development Web products and services. Based on the popularity of the web site and its associated e-mail discussion group, the SDCN decided to expand the service in spring 2001. The network invited an additional eight organizations to attend a workshop in Vancouver to draft an expanded resource kit. In addition to attracting new members to the SDCN, these activities attracted additional funding and participation from CIDA and the World Bank Institute. In summer 2001, the SDCN began to develop proposals to share their expertise and to involve additional networks and organizations in improving civil society Web communication practices through a broader training and peer networking initiative.

Our findings based on the behaviour of not-for-profit research networks parallel those within the private sector. Recent research on innovation by Michael Schrage at the Massachusetts Institute of Technology (MIT) challenges traditional assumptions about teams.[82] Contrary to popular belief that innovative teams generate innovative prototypes, innovative prototypes in fact generate innovative teams. As Schrage has discovered, "an interesting prototype emits the social and intellectual equivalent of a magnetic field, attracting smart people with interesting ideas about how to make it better."[83] Good prototypes reveal underlying assumptions and create a demand for shared spaces (real or virtual) for conversation about them.

One implication of the prototype approach is that it is acceptable, even recommendable, to have strong lead organizations for projects and the network as a whole. These organizations will propose ideas, structures and processes for other members to consider and revise.

In theory, excellent sustainable development pilot projects should attract excellent staff and continued funding. Unfortunately, this is not always the case. Unlike in the private sector, success does not always attract continued support. Development fashions and trends may shift funding away from successful projects before the teams have matured sufficiently to be able to implement projects and to seek additional resources and contacts. This is especially difficult for virtual teams since they may require more time to build trust and shared ways of working. However, if the network can agree upon guidelines for the network project development process during its initial set-up phase (within the first one or two years), it will be better positioned to succeed in attracting future project funding.

Managing the collective project and proposal development process can be seen as the most critical activity of a knowledge network. The more network governance and membership are structured around the conscious creation of collaborative projects, the greater the likelihood of the network's innovation and success. However this is not a task for the faint of heart. It requires unprecedented levels of honesty and transparency at all levels between organizations.

Network teams must address the following issues regarding project proposal development:

- Who is responsible for developing new product ideas?
- How will these ideas be presented to other members of the knowledge network?
- How does the individual with the idea begin to gather a project team?
- How will the initial project team prototype a proposal? Within what time frames?
- How will the project team determine that a proposal is ready to be shared with external audiences and funders for further revision?
- What funds should be budgeted for the team leader and for other team members for process support?
- Who will raise funds for the project?

Contract and financial management

Most literature on virtual teams assumes that teams are primarily comprised of individuals from within the same large corporation. No mention is made of the difficulties of financial management and budgeting within virtual teams across organizations. However, this can often be a major challenge for CSOs undertaking knowledge network projects.

Knowledge networks must grapple with the following issues:

- Equity – Since organizations in various parts of the world face different cost structures and have varying staff availability to contribute to a project, it is highly unlikely that all will receive the same amount of funding for participation in a particular project.
- Scale – Funding must be of a level adequate to attract and maintain the commitment of each member organization to the project. While a project may be $100,000 overall, if there are four organizations participating, each will only receive a portion of the funds.
- Transaction costs – While there are internal incentives for an organization to serve as project lead clearing all project funds through the organization's books, the benefits to other participating institutions can be considerably less. At a certain point, the transaction costs for each organization to process financial transfers may outweigh the benefits to them of participation. On occasion, SDCN network organizations have requested that staff work on small (CAD$2,000) project contracts as individual consultants with funds paid directly to the staff member.
- Multiple currencies – Shorter project cycles may help to minimize potential problems with fluctuating exchange rates. Nevertheless, project managers will have to cope with amalgamating financial reports from project participants in multiple currencies.
- Currency restrictions – A broader problem in dealing with international currencies is the existence of restrictions on funds being sent out of specific countries. Banking restrictions in some countries place prohibitive costs on the agencies there if they needed to send project funds to other sustainable development institutions around the world.
- Contracting cultures – Some sustainable development institutions follow standardized or generally accepted accounting procedures to account for the receipt of funds from donors as well

as how funds have been expended and redistributed to other contracted project partners. Other institutions have more informal systems in place whereby fewer documents may be required.

Given the high opportunity costs for negotiating financial/contracting procedures for each project, the network should develop contract templates and financial procedures that can be modified to suit individual network projects. These templates and procedures will generally follow the accounting/contracting practices of the strictest member. Given that membership and institutional practices may change over time, the network should review contracting procedures periodically. In this way, knowledge networks can be seen as a force moving towards the standardization of international civil society.

Implementing

When properly managed, collaborative projects are capable of creating and managing new kinds of relationships within and outside a knowledge network. Through shaping a shared proposal development and implementation process, a knowledge network answers the question "What kind of interactions do we want to create?"[84] Project-focused interactions are at the heart of knowledge networks. How they are managed will determine the character, energy, creativity and success of the knowledge network.

Process management involves resolving key issues including:

- How will the project team decide which person and which organization will lead the project team for the implementation phase?
- How will the project be evaluated?
- Who are the team members that will need to be involved? At what stages in the process?
- How will team members be welcomed into the group? How will it be clearly communicated that their work is complete?
- Who is responsible for each task/action that needs to be undertaken?
- How will timelines be established and agreed to?
- By what criteria will work be accepted as complete and of sufficient quality?
- What formats and forums will be used for discussion and feedback of prototype products?

- What will happen when a team member misses a deadline?
- How will copyright and proprietary information be handled?
- What acknowledgement and credits must be extended to team members, their organizations, the network and funders?
- How will the project conclude?
- How will the project team extract lessons from the process for feedback to the broader network?

These types of questions force individuals and institutions to confront the tyranny of trade-offs. That confrontation, in turn, forces people to play seriously with the difficult choices they must ultimately make.[85]

Most staff do not work solely on the activities of a particular knowledge network. With the increasing complexity of projects and skills sets required for their effective implementation, CSOs tend to spread staff across many projects. The result is that most research staff are responsible for leading and participating in a variety of project teams within their organization at any given time. If the organization is a member of one or more knowledge networks, staff will also be managing their schedules to determine how best to meet complex schedules and deadlines.

As the number of projects and institutions dealt with by any individual increases, their ability to successfully complete all tasks can often be compromised. Frequently, knowledge network projects receive lower priority in a person's complex scheduling. This may occur for many reasons:

- funding received by their institution for a network project may be lower than for single-institution projects;
- they feel that their supervisor does not see the effort put into the network project, and therefore might not not be considered in personal evaluations and recommendations; and
- CSOs frequently operate in crisis mode—feelings of urgency are usually more intense when project staff are in the same physical location.

Functional cultures

Knowledge networks must draw on the skills of staff from different functional areas of each member organization. Project managers, researchers, administrative assistants, communications specialists, information technology managers and accountants may all be part of a virtual project team at any given time. However, each functional group may share common ways of working, shared vocabularies and assumptions about project management. Conflicts may occur in virtual teams when people from different functions disagree about how appropriate a particular approach is.

In sustainable development knowledge networks, one example of a functional culture clash is that which may occur between researchers and communications specialists. Communications staff frequently complain that they are considered second-class staff within their institutions and that their skill sets are undervalued. On the other side, researchers frequently complain that communication staff take too long to complete their tasks and create a bottleneck in the production and release of timely research. In addition to differences in education and professional socialization, these conflicts may also be exacerbated by gender and age differences between research and communications staff. Training sessions on the organization's communications practices and/or developing communications steering committees may reduce conflicts to some degree.

Crossing technical boundaries

Knowledge networks have a wide variety of real and virtual spaces within which to collaborate on the development of projects. All may be necessary at some point in the development of collaborative projects.

Before exploring technical options open to knowledge networks, it is important to note that face-to-face meetings are by far the best forum for interaction and collaborative work. They are context-rich and allow for the most direct resolution of conflicts and miscommunications. Unfortunately, knowledge networks rarely have the travel funds to do all the work in person. In addition, many sustainable development organizations are trying to reduce travel in efforts to "walk the talk" of sustainability. Some degree of electronic communication will therefore have to be used at various points in the conceptualization and implementation of a project.

The challenge is to match an available technology with the team's task at any given point in time. Two primary factors can help virtual teams to assess the effectiveness of one technology over another in different situations:[86]

1. Social presence – Social presence is the degree to which the technology facilitates a personal connection with others. Synchronous (same-time) communications have higher social presence than asynchronous (different time) communications because they enable a spontaneous, back-and-forth exchange.

Situations that are ambiguous or ill-defined or that require the expression of emotions call for a technology with high social presence. Routine situations, such as regular exchanges of information, may benefit from technologies with less social presence.

2. Information richness – Information richness has to do with the amount and variety of information flowing through a particular communication medium. High information richness helps to accurately transfer clues to the meaning of the communication, thereby reducing confusion and misunderstanding.

Other factors that should be considered include: the ability to generate a permanent record of the communication, time constraints, access to technological training and support, organizational and functional cultures, and experience and familiarity with virtual operations.

The following section reviews some of the learnings from IISD's knowledge networks on organizing and facilitating these collaborative spaces for network management and project teams. For additional information on matching tools to situations, *Mastering Virtual Teams*[87] will serve as an invaluable resource. In addition, *Working Together Online*[88] provides in-depth advice on how to facilitate virtual communities and work groups.

Telephone

The telephone is perhaps the most familiar collaborative technology for virtual teams. It is also one of the most effective tools, especially for maintaining contact between members of network management virtual teams. Phone calls provide high levels of social presence and information richness that maintain stronger relationships at the core of the network. Phone calls are also the best tool for resolving conflicts or for sharing sensitive information. People are willing to say many more things than they would write down about how the organization operates and what internal challenges a project may be facing.

Conference calls are useful throughout the implementation of projects and activities. At the beginning of a project, a conference call enables team members to establish a sense of themselves as a team. Hearing each other's voices adds an additional dimension to the relationship and lends a small force to ensuring a sense of mutual responsibility and obligation to people. Should scheduling conflicts arise during project implementation, a conference call can provide the venue for the team to regroup and re-establish priorities. At the end of a project, conference calls can enable the quick brainstorming of lessons learned. Learning is a group activity and is most easily undertaken when the insights of one member can spark additional thoughts from the others. Group debriefing is especially important for knowledge networks since members of a project team can anticipate working with each other in the future in other project teams. Problems and conflicts must be dealt with in a respectful and appreciative manner in order to ensure that mistakes will not be repeated in the future and organizations feel comfortable continuing to work together. Conference calls help to minimize misunderstandings during these group-learning sessions.

Tips:

- Conference calls with many international partners may require up to two weeks to organize. This provides ample time to ensure the availability of team members and to double check their phone numbers. Sustainable development staff travel frequently and may not be at their home office during the time of a call. Nevertheless, if scheduled in advance, team members may be able to join the call from a hotel phone anywhere in the world.
- Conference calls for a virtual team should be held at a regular time and consistently communicated in reference to a selected time zone. The SDCN found that one-hour long calls starting at 13:00 GMT were the most effective for its network management team with members spread from Costa Rica to India. Invitations should include reference to standard time zone converters[89] in order to assist members to calculate their local time. Even with a consistent reference time, local call times may vary due to daylight savings time.
- Shop around for conference call rates. One of the most useful aspects of a knowledge network is its distributed geography. Given lower teleconferencing rates in Canada than in developing regions, IISD has convened a number of project team conference calls for other SDCN members, even when IISD was not directly involved in the project. This has proven cost-effective.
- It is advisable to use a commercial teleconferencing service for conference calls involving more than three people. While it may be more expensive than in-house options, it frees the team leader and participants to focus on the objectives of the call while the operator handles technical difficulties. Most commercial services will provide a toll-free number to each call participant to contact if they are accidentally disconnected from the call.
- The final versions of the agenda and supporting documents for a conference call should ideally be circulated at least two days

prior to the call to enable members to print them out and review them. Depending on time limits and number of call participants, the agenda should be restricted to one or two major issues with decisions.

- Each call will require one or two people to act as moderators. One person should be focused on facilitating the conversation to ensure that issues are covered and that all team members have had an opportunity to participate. This person should check regularly for feedback from quieter members of the team. The second person should serve as note-taker to ensure that suggestions are captured and wording of any decision is clear. Depending on the size of the group and the nature of the issue under discussion, it may be difficult for one person to play both roles.
- Conference call minutes should be typed up and circulated to call participants by e-mail to check their accuracy before being shared with others.

E-mail

E-mail is the most often used communication tool for knowledge network virtual teams. Its asynchronous nature allows members to communicate with each other when and where it is most convenient for them. E-mail messages can either be sent directly from one team member to another or through a discussion group from one person to all team members. A combination of each is usually necessary throughout a project.

Team-based e-mail discussion groups are invaluable tools for discussion and document circulation. There are many platforms available that organizations may either purchase (e.g., Lyris) or customize and use (e.g., Yahoo Groups). The decision between these options should be based on the availability of technical staff within the network as well as the level of comfort a group has with using a commercial service. Increasingly, knowledge networks are finding the free Web applications[90] can provide the same or better level of quality service as ones you must purchase and configure in house.

Tips:

- Find out if any team members use alternate e-mail addresses when travelling. Staff within organizations without much technical support may maintain multiple e-mail accounts, using a Hotmail or other free Web-based e-mail account while on the road.

- In addition to a general closed discussion group for all relevant staff within the knowledge network's member organizations, establish one closed discussion group per virtual team. The general list should be used for general discussions and information sharing. The team lists are for more specific conversations regarding each project.
- Adhere to standard netiquette and do not forward messages from one list to another without the explicit approval of the message's original author. At the same time, assume that anything you write may "accidentally" be forwarded to others. Do not write anything in an e-mail that you would not wish everyone in the network to read.

Online chat

Online chats provide an opportunity for multiple people to send text messages to each other in real time. However, given time zone differences and unequal technological support, online chat meetings can be difficult. To this point, we have not considered it to be an appropriate technology for any of IISD's knowledge network virtual teams. However, we did use it with one virtual team of young people working on a prep conference leading up to Global Knowledge 2000. The steering committee of seven young people from Malaysia, India, Kenya, Costa Rica, Colombia and Canada used a free online chat service to hold a two-hour meeting finalizing plans for an e-conference.

Tips:

- Like a conference call, special attention must be given to establishing a clear agenda and to ensuring that team members know the local time of the meeting.
- Chat meetings require roughly twice as long as conference call meetings to cover the same agenda. People type much more slowly than they speak. Agendas must be correspondingly shorter.
- The moderator of a chat meeting should prepare statements introducing each agenda item in advance of the meeting. These can be quickly cut and pasted into the chat dialogue window at appropriate times.
- Delays between participants beginning to type and finishing can lead to staggered, incomprehensible threading of the chat. To avoid this, the moderator should ask who has a comment to make and then call on people in order to type/submit their

comments. This helps to ensure that comments are not repeated and the discussion builds upon earlier comments.

Online video/audio conferencing

Online video/audio conferencing has been touted for many years as a cost-saving forum for virtual team meetings. While NetMeeting is increasingly available to organizations as they upgrade to new versions of Microsoft Office software, it has proven to be of limited utility for sustainable development virtual teams scattered around the world. More time is often spent on technical adjustments than on the substance of the meeting.

In our experience, the most useful application of audio/video conferencing so far has been in conjunction with face-to-face meetings. The representative from the Earth Council to the SDCN was unable to attend a network meeting in Canada in December 1997 in person. He joined instead through NetMeeting from his office in Costa Rica. Six months later, the representative from the Stockholm Environment Institute used NetMeeting to participate in a network meeting held in Costa Rica. In May 1999, we attempted to have a representative from the Canadian International Development Agency participate through NetMeeting in a workshop held in Dakar, Senegal. Heavy network traffic and poor quality connections negated the effectiveness of that experiment.

From these experiences, we found that it was necessary to have one support staff at the physical meeting location assigned to monitoring the NetMeeting connection. This person needed to continuously ensure that the audio feed in each direction was clear. Video was of poor quality and was disabled as soon as a clear image of the person could be captured and stored. The technician would also maintain contact with the remote participant through the chat feature of NetMeeting. If the remote participant wished to make a comment or intervention in the meeting, the technician would indicate this to the rest of the room.

Extranets

Extranets are controlled access Web spaces for members of a knowledge network or one of its project teams. The main function of extranets has been storage of common project information—databases of members and their contact information and space to upload files. From our experience, few team members either upload or download information from team extranets. Nevertheless, they may serve as an important historical reference for the network, supporting the orientation of new staff at member organizations.

Collaborative Internet software

There are a growing number of companies providing specialized software for virtual team collaboration. These collaboration platforms integrate many of the online features outlined above with tools for sending group e-mails, chat, uploading documents and managing group calendars and tasks. More advanced platforms allow the creation of shared whiteboards, document version control, shared Web navigating and sharing of desktop control. Some of this software is Web-based (e.g., YahooGroups, CommunityZero, WebEx); other applications require the download and installation of specialized software (e.g., Groove, NetMeeting). Some companies (e.g., Eroom) provide both options depending on the desired level of use and functionality. Most companies provide a basic level of service for free and charge for additional storage space or features. Of these services, YahooGroups, CommunityZero and Groove appear to provide the best range of options for not-for-profit sustainable development teams.

Nevertheless, we have not found collaborative Internet software tools to be useful for knowledge networks. While they may be well-designed, there is little demand by team leaders or team members for the services the advanced features they provide. This reflects more on the informality of civil society project management styles than it does on the software itself.

Conclusion

In the spirit of innovation and prototyping, IISD has established several knowledge networks over the past three years. These networks have spawned collaborative projects created and implemented by virtual teams. We have found that leadership of the management and project teams is one of the most critical indicators of long-term network success. This leadership demonstrates itself through the establishment of consistent procedures for teams that allow them to contribute their skills and knowledge. These procedures will reflect the nature of network activities as well as the national, organizational and functional cultures of the organizations involved.

Endnotes

70 Blau, Andrew. *More Than Bit Players: How Information Technology Will Change the Ways Nonprofits and Foundations Work and Thrive in the Information Age.* Surdna Foundation. http://www.surdna.org/documents/morefinal.pdf (May 2001)

71 Additional information about the CCKN is available online at http://www.cckn.net/.

72 Additional information about the TKN can be found online at http://www.iisd.org/tkn/.

73 Additional information about the SDCN can be found online at http://www.sdcn.org/.

74 Lipnack, Jessica and Jeffrey Stamps. *Virtual Teams: Reaching Across Space, Time and Organizations with Technology*. John Wiley and Sons, Inc: New York, 1997. p. 6–7.

75 Duarte, Deborah L. and Nancy Tennant Snyder. *Mastering Virtual Teams: Strategies, Tools, and Techniques That Succeed.* Jossey-Bass Publishers: San Francisco, 1999. p. 10.

76 Weinberger, David. "Groupthink: Collaboration as Conversation." *ePulse*. http://www.eroom.com/epulse/epulse_groupthink.asp (July 24, 2001).

77 Duarte and Snyder, p. 54.

78 Duarte and Snyder, p. 56.

79 Duarte and Snyder, p. 56–8.

80 Duarte and Snyder, p. 63.

81 Schrage, Michael. *Serious Play: How the World's Best Companies Simulate to Innovate*. Boston: Harvard Business School Press, 2000. p. 71.

82 Schrage, p. 71.

83 Schrage, p. 28.

84 Schrage, p. 20.

85 Schrage, p. 20.

86 Duarte and Snyder, p. 26.

87 Duarte and Snyder.

88 Rykert, Liz and Maureen James. *Working Together Online*. Web Networks: Toronto, 1997.

89 http://www.worldtimezone.com/time24.htm and http://www.worldtimeserver.com/ are among the services available online.

90 Free services are usually supported by advertising. If your virtual team does not wish to be subjected to advertising in each e-mail and on the Web interface, you may pay roughly US$50 per year to have the advertising removed.

Chapter 6
Measuring While You Manage: Planning, monitoring and evaluating knowledge networks

The challenge of network evaluation

In this book, we have:

- articulated several operating principles for networks;
- recommended approaches for engaging decision-makers through networks;
- reviewed the creation and management of relationships within networks; and
- discussed some of the mechanics of virtual collaboration and communications among members.

We often refer to what we see as the "network advantage" over other individual or collaborative approaches to change. Knowledge networks:

- emphasize joint value creation by all the members within the network (moving beyond the sharing of information to the aggregation and creation of new knowledge);
- strengthen capacity for research and communications in all members in the network; and
- identify and implement strategies to engage decision-makers more directly, linking to appropriate processes, and moving the network's knowledge into policy and practice. Partner organizations bring with them their own contacts and spheres of influence, thereby extending the reach and influence of all partners to a wider range of decision-makers.

This chapter takes a closer look at the evaluation of networks. In particular, we hope to provide some insight into how to monitor and assess whether the network advantage is being realized.

While the literature on institutional planning, development project evaluation and social marketing is rich, extensive and almost overwhelming, we have found very little specifically related to monitoring and evaluating the performance of networks. In our own networks and in several others, we have observed a number of significant difficulties with planning and evaluation.

Network evaluation, when it takes place, is usually driven by requirements to report to funders on whether goals and objectives have been achieved. Depending on the financial model for the network, reports are required for:

- a large grant from one or two donors, which has been provided to a lead institution to cover all network activities; and
- specific project funds from a variety of donors, that have been granted to individual members for individual projects, or to groups of members for joint projects.

When a large grant to cover all the costs of network activities is being sought, the lead institution often defaults to more traditional project planning and evaluation methodologies when preparing the grant proposal. The methodology selected may be required by the prospective funder. Usually, the lead institution sets the framework in consultation with the funder and assesses the performance of its peers in the network within that framework. This leads to several problems:

- The lead institution treats the network as a single project among many projects managed by the institution. Consequently, in evaluation, the institution looks at specific project deliverables, rather than at the value of the relationships that have emerged from working collaboratively. The network advantage—joint value creation, mutual capacity development and collective engagement of decision-makers—which results from those relationships, goes unmeasured and unvalued.
- Rarely does the lead institution review its own performance as a member of the network.
- Rarely are the members involved in joint discussions around what they think might be indicators of success for network activities. What is eventually achieved by individual members might turn out to be quite different over time from what the lead institution speculated in the grant proposal. But, because the organizer is tied to a pre-set assessment framework, those achievements might go unrecognized because there is no process in place to capture and report on them.

The second financial model leads to additional problems. As a network grows and matures, the members will manage many different projects, supported by different funders. The cumulative cost of detailed evaluation of the full range of network projects can be prohibitively high. The members leading individual projects report on results to their own funders, often without sharing the evaluation with other members. No opportunity is available to aggregate the individual successes to see whether the network as a whole is really fulfilling its potential, or whether it is simply a convenient umbrella for a set of projects run by a number of organizations.

Whether there is a single grant or a number of project grants, current evaluation practices rarely provide opportunities for the network members to learn from each other about what is working well in their activities, about whether the network is having the influence it wishes to have, and about what needs to be adjusted during the funding contribution period.

The case for evaluating networks

We believe that networks need to be evaluated on the effectiveness of the network (doing the right thing) and the efficiency of the network (doing things right).

1. The effectiveness of the network (doing the right things)

   In a network supported by only one or two major grants, there is a certain cohesiveness of objectives that makes it somewhat easier to monitor whether the network is building capacity, creating joint value and influencing policy processes. This becomes much more difficult when the network is supported by a variety of grants for a variety of projects within the network. Nevertheless, in both cases it is necessary to find the means to demonstrate the value-added of the network approach, for three reasons:

   a. Formal knowledge networks come together to leverage change in policies and practices, supportive of sustainable development. A network needs to be able to determine what changes it has effected through its research and communications work. It needs to monitor whether it is fully realizing its "network advantage." This requires a methodology that not only assesses individual activities, but provides some means for identifying changes as a result of its combination of efforts.

   b. Value-added propositions—ones that demonstrate real leverage of money and influence—are highly attractive to funders. Networks need to be able to make the case that operating in a network mode does lead to focused collaboration, better informed research results, new knowledge and real influence.

   c. Networks often require a great deal of in-kind support from member institutions, especially during gaps in specific project funding. The network coordinators need to be able to demonstrate to the members that it is worth the additional investment of time and effort in order to sustain network momentum over the long term.

2. The efficiency of the network (doing things right)

   This point is often overlooked in traditional evaluation frameworks, and yet over and over we hear about the transactional costs of networks:

   - the management of relationships is cumbersome and time-consuming
   - the motivation and performance of individual members is often at issue
   - the cost effectiveness of the network approach is in question.

   The last point is the most controversial. Does a funder see more results, more quickly by donating $200,000 to each of five organizations to carry out research on a given issue or by giving $1 million to a network of five organizations? And yet, in spite of these ongoing challenges to the network approach, networks rarely put in place the means to monitor, review and adjust the internal operations of the network.

The purpose of this chapter is to highlight current approaches, identify the elements most useful in those approaches for networks, and develop our experimental framework for planning, monitoring and evaluation. This is an area requiring more research, more experimentation and more implementation of executable monitoring and evaluation frameworks. This chapter may raise more questions than solutions at this stage of our research.

Overview of available methodologies

We have scanned several of the most common project planning and evaluation approaches:

- SWOT analysis (strengths, weaknesses, opportunities, threats);
- Results-based management;
- Logical framework analysis;
- Outcome mapping; and
- Appreciative inquiry.

There are some similarities among these approaches:

- they are all intended to be planning tools, as well as project monitoring and evaluation tools. The evaluation components are embedded in the plan from the beginning;
- they should all be participatory, with input coming from all those involved in the project;
- several provide for the identification of qualitative and quantitative indicators of success;
- some anticipate some form of regular monitoring throughout the life of the project, although only outcome mapping actually prescribes a monitoring approach; and
- most require some form of evaluation report at the end of the project, either looking back over the project, forward to future activities or both.

In looking at the most common approaches, we observed that none drew from lessons in the field of human resources performance evaluation. Since networks are about relationships, we thought it useful to also look at evaluation methods from the human resources field. We were delighted to find many of the elements needed for network evaluation that were sometimes lacking in other evaluation methods: simplicity, learning/feedback loops, and the ability to acknowledge and address the unexpected.

Table 9. A cursory overview of common planning and evaluation techniques.

Technique	Description
SWOT analysis	**Context:** Used by marketers in the private sector to assess the performance of current product lines and openings for new products. Used by organizations in strategic planning to assess current activities and directions for new activities. It can be used as a gap analysis tool—where an organization is today, and where it needs to be tomorrow.

<table>
<tr><th>Technique</th><th>Description</th></tr>
<tr><td></td><td>
Core elements:
It requires a participatory process. By filling in a simple grid, planners can collaboratively highlight internal capabilities and external factors.
<table>
<tr><th></th><th>Positive</th><th>Negative</th></tr>
<tr><td>Internal</td><td>Strengths</td><td>Weaknesses</td></tr>
<tr><td>External</td><td>Opportunities</td><td>Threats</td></tr>
</table>
Using strengths and opportunities, planners can assess whether to initiate or continue with a product or activity, and mitigate against apparent weaknesses and threats.
</td></tr>
<tr><td>Results-based management (RBM)</td><td>
Context:
Used by development practitioners to plan and monitor projects. Focuses project managers on short, mid-term and long-term development results. Considers a result as a describable or measurable change resulting from a cause and effect relationship.

Core elements:
The results chain:
Project → Output → Outcome → Impact
<table>
<tr><th>Inputs</th><th>Activities</th><th>Outputs</th><th>Outcomes</th><th>Impacts</th></tr>
<tr><td>Money, staff.</td><td>What you will do, with whom you will work.</td><td>Short-term results/ products, (within one year of a project) affecting individuals.</td><td>Mid-term accompl-ishments (by the end of the project) affecting organizations [corresponds to logical framework analysis purpose level].</td><td>Long-term results: what you would like to see happen as a result of the project [corresponds to logical framework analysis goal level].</td></tr>
<tr><td colspan="2">Operational Results</td><td colspan="3">Development Results</td></tr>
</table>
Usually developed by project proponent and donor, without input from project partners, using a framework prescribed by the donor.
</td></tr>
</table>

Technique	Description
Logical framework analysis (LFA)	**Context:** Used by development practitioners to plan and monitor projects. Requires project planners to be clear and specific about the project, its objectives, obstacles and results. The LFA is a key tool in Results-based management. **Core elements:**

	Description	Indicators	Means of verification	Underlying assumptions/ risks
Goal				
Purpose				
Outputs				
Activities				

Technique	Description
Outcome mapping	**Context:** Developed by the International Development Research Centre. Recognizes that within the RBM/LFA approaches: • there is an implied causality to project work that is not necessarily true: a desired goal or result may be achieved but there may be other factors leading to that result; • that results or goals may not be seen until some time after the life of the project. • that the "outcome" component in these approaches is often not well understood by users. Draws from the social marketing field the emphasis on behaviour change, reflected in changes in activities and relationships. Concentrates on "outcomes" as changes in behaviour, relationships, activities/actions in those with whom the project works directly. Introduces grades of change: what would the assessor want or expect to see a partner change; what would they like to see, and what would they love to see. Provides a methodology for defining who partners are; and for mapping progress towards outcomes as a more reasonable indication of a project's success. Acknowledges that anecdotal information (stories), if collected systematically over time, can provide a reliable indication of desired changes and outcomes.

<table>
<tr><th>Technique</th><th>Description</th></tr>
<tr><td></td><td>Core elements:
<table>
<tr><td>Intentional design</td><td>Why (vision)
Who (boundary partners)
What (outcome challenges and progress markers)
How (strategy maps)</td></tr>
<tr><td>Outcome and performance monitoring</td><td>Systematized self-assessment:
Journals for recording progress marker, strategy performance</td></tr>
<tr><td>Evaluation planning</td><td>Review of project</td></tr>
</table>
Can be developed in consultation with project partners.</td></tr>
<tr><td>Appreciative inquiry (AI)</td><td>Context:
Developed by Case Western Reserve as a process for identifying the positive within a company—strengths and successes—and focusing the energy of the company on pursuing the positive. AI is one of many participatory evaluation methodologies.

As with outcome mapping, stories become the indicators of success.

Core elements:
The four "D" cycle:
<table>
<tr><td>Discover</td><td>Identifying what is working well and where the energy in an organization lies:
• participants each describe best experiences within the organization; and
• participants describe what they value most in themselves, in their work and in the organization.</td></tr>
<tr><td>Dream</td><td>Participants look to the future:
• what would they consider to be a success for the organization?; and
• what would they like to see for themselves, their work, their organization?</td></tr>
<tr><td>Design</td><td>Participants scope out a plan of work based on what they have discovered about their strengths, values and visions.</td></tr>
<tr><td>Delivery</td><td>Participants execute the plan.</td></tr>
</table></td></tr>
</table>

<table>
<tr><th>Technique</th><th>Description</th></tr>
<tr><td>Human resource performance evaluation frameworks (HR)</td><td>
Context:
Most organizations have a process for reviewing and evaluating the performance of individual staff members on an annual basis. The key is regular, systematic assessment of activities against a clear terms of reference for the staff member.

The objectives of the process are to:
• recognize success and identify ways to address problems;
• identify strengths and potential contributions not formerly recognized;
• create a learning cycle, from one year to the next; and
• do so in a fair, objective manner.

Core elements:
<table>
<tr><td>Terms of reference</td><td>Description of the position and tasks to be undertaken. Individual to be assessed on performance of those tasks.</td></tr>
<tr><td>Grading assessment</td><td>A simple rating for each task, usually from 1 to 4:
1. Does not meet expectations;
2. Occasionally meets expectations
3. Consistently meets expectations
4. Exceeds expectations</td></tr>
<tr><td>Descriptive assessment</td><td>Short examples (stories) of individual's accomplishments or challenges for each task.</td></tr>
<tr><td>Future expectations set</td><td>A statement of where performance needs improvement and how that will be achieved; a statement of new goals and expectations.</td></tr>
</table>
There are often common elements or "job parts" in performance evaluation frameworks, for example:
• substantive/technical knowledge;
• project management and supervision;
• communications with stakeholders;
• new project development and fundraising; and
• contribution to institutional planning.

Evaluation is always conducted jointly by three parties: the independent HR manager, the immediate supervisor and the staff person.
</td></tr>
</table>

Frameworks for network planning, monitoring and evaluation

In order to create what we hope might be a simpler, but useful approach for network assessment, we have taken components from the various methodologies available to design our experimental frameworks.

We have taken from outcome mapping four key components:

1. The sequence of planning, monitoring and evaluation. We have attempted to reduce the number of steps involved in order to provide a simpler, more executable process for small and mid-sized networks with limited staff and resources.

2. Outcome mapping's core premise, that the emphasis in project evaluation should be on identifying outcomes as changes in behaviours, actions and relationships.

3. Its recognition that it is the people in the network, including the network coordinator, who will change their own activities, behaviours and relationships as a result of working together. In outcome mapping, the "boundary partners" are primarily the network members themselves, although in outcome mapping, each boundary partner in a major program such as a network can have its own boundary partners. To avoid confusion between levels of boundary partners, we have chosen instead to use the term "stakeholders": those individuals and groups outside of the core group of partners in the network, which the network wants to influence. Some would call this the "target audience," although we prefer not to use that term as it conveys an image of receivers of messages rather than those engaged in action.

4. Its core methodology, that stories recorded systematically over time can provide a reliable indication of changes, and therefore outcomes, brought about through network activities.

From results-based management, we have adopted the distinctions between operational results and development results. "Development results" correspond to our "network effectiveness" or "doing the right thing." We consider that "operational results" are an outcome of "network efficiency" or "doing things right."

From logical framework analysis we have recognized the importance of metrics and indicators. We reflect in our frameworks the points at which those are captured, and how they are determined. As a tool for measuring outputs, we continue to be interested in how we might make better use of Web traffic statistics, imperfect as they are, to provide broad indicators of levels of use of products and services coming from networks. [91]

From human resource management, we have taken the concept of annual evaluations with a grading component and an anecdotal report, as well as the emphasis on revision of plans and expectations based on performance.

Using these components, we have created three frameworks:

1. Planning: used at the beginning of network activities to record the work plan, the beneficiaries of the work (partners and stakeholders) and the indicators of change desired:
    - for major projects or programs within the network; and
    - for the network as a whole.
2. Monitoring: used quarterly, to track activities.
3. Evaluation:
    - Annual:
        1. used to assess whether the network's programs are on track, whether anticipated outcomes are being achieved and whether adjustments need to be made in activities; and
        2. used to assess whether the network as a whole is realizing its potential:
            - Is the network linking effectively to relevant policy processes; is the level of recognition and influence of the network and its members increasing within these circles?
            - Are members adding value to each others' work, and creating new work together that might not have happened otherwise?
            - Is there an exchange and building of capacity across the network membership?
    - End of project evaluation: used to aggregate information to report to the donor.

Planning framework

In Chapter 4, we outlined the requirements for setting goals, objectives and work plans for a network. The key point in the process is the need to establish a work plan for the network as a whole. Many networks tend to keep work plans at the individual project level. While the individual projects may be highly successful, they may not serve to drive forward the broader strategic intention of the network. The network plan would at the very least aggregate the individual project plans, in order to monitor timelines, budgets, deliverables and the implementation of communications strategies for each project. But the network plan would also encompass the bigger picture: the checkpoints for reviewing progress on strategic intent and the stages for building relationships with decision-makers.

Planning a network has two stages: first, the development of the concept, the proposal and the securing of start-up grants; and second, the first meeting at which the new members get together to discuss what they are going to do together.

Stage 1: Proposal development

This stage is largely dictated by the interests of the dominant partner(s), the prospects for funding and by the planning and evaluation framework required by the most likely funder. The lead institution(s) traditionally determines the goal, but can (and probably should) refine this in consultation with potential network members. Our primary advice at this stage is to review the planning framework below, as it may influence or clarify the identification of outcomes in the proposal.

Stage 2: The first network meeting

We have observed over a number of years that network meetings tend to follow the same patterns of discussion. There are always three key issues under debate:

1. whether members are still in agreement with the goals and objectives to which they have committed previously among themselves or with the funders;
2. substantive discussions on the work itself; and
3. logistics on how the work will get done.

Given limited time and the members' desire to focus on substantive work and financial matters, it is unlikely that most networks will ever be inclined to allocate a day or more for either Outcome Mapping or Appreciative Inquiry approaches to monitoring and evaluation. We have therefore drafted a planning session that is responsive to how members normally behave in a network meeting. The key to our approach is the weaving into the substantive discussion the four questions which are often overlooked at network meetings:

1. what can members contribute to, as well as receive from, the network;

2. what will success look like for the network as a whole;
3. for each activity, who is going to benefit, be changed or influenced by the work; and
4. what will be the indicators of success for each activity?

In its simplest form, the process is as follows:

a) When the network meets, the first item on the agenda should be a review of the goals of the network as stated in the project documents. Members should then consider their own views for the vision, mission and objectives of the network as a whole. Objectives for their participation should include what they hope to contribute to the network (to other members and to the network itself). The chair/facilitator/network coordinator should ask members for their views on what success will look like for the network. The refined views on goals, objectives and measures of success for the network are recorded by the coordinator for revisiting at the time of network evaluation.

b) When members begin to discuss individual projects, they are asked by the chair/facilitator/network coordinator:

   - how they see themselves benefiting from the project, what they expect to learn or gain from it; and
   - who else will benefit from the project, be changed or influenced by the work.

c) At the end of the substantive discussion of the project, members are asked for indicators of success. Again, the beneficiaries and indicators are recorded by the coordinator, for revisiting as part of monitoring and evaluating the network.

This simple approach was partially and informally tested at the inaugural meeting of the Integrated Management Node of Canada's Ocean Management Research Network One project, community-based monitoring, was selected for testing. Right at the outset of discussions, members were asked who they most wanted to influence through their work. Initially, members discussed general audiences—government and government funding agencies—in broad terms. However, as the discussion progressed into the substantive areas, the members themselves kept returning to the question of influence. This led to a refinement of the research questions and the research outcomes. These were, among others, to:

- bring forward what each member in the activity area already knows about community-based monitoring (CBM) and develop a common framework to assess the various CBM approaches for members' use. (Indicators: individual contributions; participation in Web discussion; and creation of framework):

- using the framework, develop a number of case studies on different CBM approaches and to create a practitioners' guide to CBM. (Indicators: contribution of case studies; members' review of case studies; creation of guide; and requests for the guide); and
- based on members' increased understanding of the range of CBM approaches, examine how to link CBM to decision-making, within communities and within relevant government departments. (Indicators: academic paper prepared).

The simple questions of influence and indicators helped to focus the discussion and led to better defined and measurable activities for the group. The next step would be to recast this information into a monitoring framework so that members can record their progress against these more specific activities and desired outcomes.

A more detailed planning framework follows.

Detailed planning framework

Table 10a. Doing the right thing: Network effectiveness.

Steps	Explanation
Step 1: What are we going to do?	This is the opportunity to sit down with all the members to revisit and refine goals and objectives as described in funding agreements, whether the agreements are for the network as a whole, or for specific projects funded within the context of the network. The purpose of the discussion is to: • seek clarity and endorsement of the overarching goal of the network; • refine specific objectives: these could be amended, enhanced or prioritized so long as they remain consistent with the goal; • seek from members what they can contribute to—and hope to gain from—participating in the network as a whole; and • seek from members a preliminary view of what success would look like for the network. This discussion may make clear several major projects or programs of work for the network.

<table>
<tr><th>Steps</th><th>Explanation</th></tr>
<tr><td></td><td>
For example, the Climate Change Knowledge Network has three objectives, but five major projects:
<table>
<tr><th>Objectives</th><th>Projects</th></tr>
<tr><td>
• to undertake collaborative research and action on issues such as the Kyoto mechanisms, adaptation to climate change and technology transfer;
• to build capacity in developing and developed countries to better understand and address climate change issues; and
• to communicate information and knowledge within and outside the network.
</td><td>
1. Climate Compendium;
2. Capacity Building for Negotiators;
3. Vulnerability and Adaptation;
4. Decentralized Renewable Energy; and
5. Kyoto Mechanisms.
</td></tr>
</table>
Process:
1. Chair leads roundtable discussion of goals, objectives.
2. Network coordinator or meeting facilitator records notes on what members view success to be, for revisiting during Step 4, on the discussion of the overarching network plan.
3. Network coordinator or meeting facilitator consolidates discussion into two to five projects.

For Project 1: Steps 2 and 3 below may need to be repeated for each of the major projects, if there are significant differences in stakeholders, activities and outcomes for each project.
</td></tr>
<tr><td>Step 2: Who are we going to influence or change?</td><td>
In a network, there are two groups that will be changed or influenced by their interaction with the network and its work:
1. the network members themselves; and
2. the stakeholders.
</td></tr>
</table>

Steps	Explanation
	Process: It is difficult to ask the question "who are we going to influence or change" at the outset of the discussion, as members usually think first in terms of their particular research interests, field projects, etc. Only after that discussion do they consider who might be the target audience for their work. But if the question is left to the end of the discussion, the members might overlook how they themselves can benefit from the work; and they may well develop activities and outputs that may not be influential or lead to change. It is our view that asking from the beginning who they expect or want to influence or change will help to focus the substantive discussion. 1. The network members themselves. Network members were chosen based on their strengths as mavens, connectors and/or salespeople.[92] They each have some measure of influence in the world. However, participation in the network can serve to strengthen the effectiveness of each member, including the dominant/lead partner. The resulting changes in their behaviours, relationships and activities can fall into any or all of three categories: a) changes in individual member activities as an outcome of network participation; b) progressive levels of interaction among network members; or c) progressive levels of effort to engage the stakeholders each member wishes to influence. **Process:** Group discussion on which members will be participating in this project. Chair asks the relevant members to present what they can contribute and hope to gain from participating in the work program. 2. The stakeholders: those individuals and groups outside of the network which the network wants to influence; those who should have a vested interest in the work of the network, with the ability to act or to influence others to act. This includes decision-makers, mavens, connectors and salespeople outside of the network. Specificity is needed in this discussion—broad categories of stakeholders (government, media and academia) will not be helpful, as it will be difficult to articulate desired outcomes as behaviour changes for broad categories. This list of stakeholders may vary for each member and for each project. • Government ministers: Which ones? Name positions. [e.g., the trade minister for Chile] • Mid-level bureaucrats: Which ones? Name positions. [e.g., the climate change negotiator for Senegal]

<table>
<tr><th>Steps</th><th>Explanation</th></tr>
<tr><td></td><td>
<ul>
<li>Private sector: CEOs or environmental managers? Multinationals or small and medium sized enterprises?</li>
<li>Journalists: For which outlets? Mainstream or alternative?</li>
<li>Top researchers: At which institutions?</li>
<li>Web communications professionals: At which organizations?</li>
</ul>
Changes in behaviours, relationships and activities of stakeholders can be determined by progressive levels of their awareness of and interaction with individual network members and with the network as a whole.

Process:

Members to develop a list of those whom they wish to influence within this project; roundtable discussion.
</td></tr>
<tr><td>Step 3:
How are we going to effect those changes?</td><td>
This is the substantive discussion of the work plan for the project.

Process:

The members will tend to focus on the details of research, field projects or other tasks. It will be the key challenge of the chair/facilitator/network coordinator to insinuate the additional questions for each activity: what are the outputs and metrics; what are the outcomes and indicators for members; what are the outcomes and indicators for the stakeholder group for this project?

<table>
<tr><th>Work plan and outputs:
Specific activities to meet objectives; metrics of deliverables on work plan.</th><th>Outcomes – Network members:
Assessing change in behaviour, relationships and activities of network members.</th><th>Outcomes – Stakeholder group:
Assessing change in behaviour, relationships and activities.</th></tr>
<tr><td>Types of activities; sample outputs, indicators:</td><td>Types of outcomes; sample indicators:</td><td>Types of outcomes; sample indicators:</td></tr>
<tr><td>• individual members undertaking new research/communications projects done under the auspices of the network, measured by the number of specific research outputs;</td><td>• members strengthening each other's work, indicated by circulating research papers to each other for comment and peer review;</td><td>• stakeholders interacting directly with network members, as indicated by the number participating actively in electronic conferences, workshop attendance and the level of representation at workshops;</td></tr>
</table>
</td></tr>
</table>

Steps	Explanation		
	• two or more members undertaking new projects or services jointly, measured by the number of products and services; • holding electronic consultations on research findings, measured by the number of public electronic conferences held and the number of participants in the e-conference; • presentations at peer-oriented conferences (professional, academic associations), measured by the number of presentations given; and • face-to-face workshops with stakeholder group, measured by the number of workshops held.	• members creating new knowledge together, indicated by co-authoring papers; and • members improving their links to policy processes, indicated by hosting of workshops with stakeholders invited and the securing of face-to-face meetings with key decision-makers.	• stakeholders approaching network members for more advice or research, indicated by the number accepting face-to-face meetings and the number of decision-makers contracting network members for further work; and • stakeholders changing activities based on network actions/outputs, as indicated by replicating workshops on their own and by preparing position papers drawing from network research.
	Repeat for additional projects before going to Step 4.		
Step 4: The network plan	Once the specific projects and research interests have been addressed, members can revisit the general objectives, and begin to consider how to capture the cumulative effect of the individual projects and whether there are activities that all members can contribute to, which help to consolidate the network as more than an umbrella for individual projects. This step should refocus members on how to realize the network advantage: joint value creation, linking to stakeholders in the policy process; capacity development across the network.		

Steps	Explanation		
	Process:		
	Work plan and outputs: Specific activities to meet objectives; metrics of deliverables on work plan.	**Outcomes – Network members:** Assessing change in behaviour, relationships and activities of network members.	**Outcomes – Stakeholder group:** Assessing change in behaviour, relationships and activities.
	Types of activities; sample outputs, indicators:	*Types of outcomes; sample indicators:*	*Types of outcomes; sample indicators:*
	• creating a network web site and public listserv to share information about network activities, measured by web site traffic and the number of listserv subscribers; • capacity development among the members in strategic communications (media, electronic communications and publishing); • identification of major events related to the interests of the network; plans for displays, side events, presentations, etc.; • development of young professionals through exchanges; measured by the number of young professionals participating in exchanges across the network; and • monitoring the activities of the network for their cumulative "network advantage."	• members sharing information with each other across the network, indicated by linking materials to web site and posting notices on listserv; • members working together on articles related to network objectives, for publication in mainstream media outlets; • members actively participating in major events to which they would not have otherwise had access; and • young researchers developing their own project proposals as a result of their interaction with the network.	• stakeholders demonstrating increased levels of interest in network activities/outputs, indicated by the number of users from stakeholder group downloading content from the web site and joining network listserv for further information; • stakeholders approaching network members for more advice or research, indicated by the number of requests for materials and the number of decision-makers contracting network members for further work; and • stakeholders hiring young professionals from network for further work.

Table 10b. Doing things right: Network efficiency.

<table>
<tr><th>Steps</th><th colspan="2">Explanation</th></tr>
<tr><td rowspan="7">Step 5:
How are we going to work together?</td><td colspan="2">Process:
Network coordinator reviews with members the internal operations of the network. This is usually the last item on a network meeting's agenda and deals largely with logistics and finances. The network coordinator should encourage members to provide some indicators of efficient operations.</td></tr>
<tr><td>Types of activity</td><td>Sample Indicators</td></tr>
<tr><td>Network meetings
• Face to face
• Virtual (electronic/ teleconferencing)</td><td>• number held, participation by members.</td></tr>
<tr><td>Institutional support</td><td>• number of institutions that sign governance agreement;
• number of presentations that network members make to their institutions; and
• number of references to the network in individual member corporate communications.</td></tr>
<tr><td>Systems and procedures</td><td>• interaction with coordinator: timely, helpful;
• completion of quarterly progress journals; and
• contract management on projects: on time, within budget.</td></tr>
<tr><td>Prospecting for new ideas, opportunities and resources (network sustainability)</td><td>• information shared on network listserv about new funding prospects and requests for proposals; and
• number of new proposals developed by members: bringing forward prospects, vetting others.</td></tr>
<tr><td>Financial efficiency</td><td>• attracting additional funds to network activities; and
• renewal of grants; and
• amount of direct financial contribution and in-kind support from member institutions for network activities.</td></tr>
</table>

Example of a network planning framework for the Climate Change Knowledge Network

Table 11a. Doing the right thing: Network effectiveness.

Steps	Notes from network discussion		
Step 1: What are we going to do?	Limited resources, knowledge and capacity in developing countries, and lack of dialogue and understanding between industrialized and developing countries, obstruct progress toward international efforts to address climate change. The Climate Change Knowledge Network aims to help address these gaps by facilitating focused research and capacity building in developing and developed countries, supportive of sustainable development. **For Project 2** Capacity building for negotiators: Achieving a robust and equitable climate treaty requires a negotiation process in which all parties have confidence and participate as equals. But fewer resources, smaller delegations and limited access to information frequently hinder a level playing field for developing countries at the climate change negotiating table.		
Step 2: Who are we going to influence or change?	a) Members: IISD, ENDA-Energie, Institute for Environmental Studies (IVM) and the Center for Sustainable Development of the Americas (CSDA) b) Stakeholders: negotiators on developing and transitional country delegations to the Conference of the Parties (COP) to the UN Framework Convention on Climate Change.		
Step 3: How are we going to effect those changes?	**Work plan activities and outputs:** Specific activities to meet objectives; metrics of deliverables	**Outcomes – Network members:** Assessing change in behaviour, relationships and activities of network members.	**Outcomes – Stakeholder group:** Assessing change in behaviour, relationships and activities of parties targeted by network members.
	• one-week training session with African negotiators; Workshop materials prepared (metrics: number of participants);	• IISD, ENDA, IVM learn how to structure and deliver this type of workshop (indicated by evaluation reports from participants);	Key outcomes: • problem recognition and acceptance of solution offered by network; stakeholders acknowledge that their resources are limited and respond positively to network efforts

Steps	Notes from network discussion		
	• three-day training session with Latin American and Caribbean negotiators; workshop materials prepared (metrics: number of participants); • publication of handbook , CD Rom, and web site version (metrics: number of books/CDs distributed; number accesses for online version); and • launch (promotional event) of book at COP-6 (number of people attending launch).	• CSDA learns how to structure and deliver this type of workshop (indicated by evaluation reports from participants); • IISD, IVM, ENDA and CSDA share experiences on regional differences in training programs; • members refine materials suitable for handbook; IISD, IVM, CSDA, ENDA strengthen each other's work through joint writing and peer review of handbook; and • members increase profile and promote expertise at key stakeholder venue.	to work with them to address the gaps; and workshop participants gain better understanding of negotiating process (on the substance and on negotiating techniques). Indicators: • Negotiators themselves attend workshop (rather than more junior staff); responses on workshop evaluation forms; responses on follow-up surveys after subsequent round of negotiations; • stakeholders endorse book (willingness to contribute to book, demand for book and recommendations to others); and • other stakeholders request similar workshops and materials for their countries/regions.

Steps	Notes from network discussion		
Step 4: The Network plan	**Work plan activities and outputs:** Specific activities to meet objectives; metrics of deliverables	**Outcomes – Network members:** Assessing change in behaviour, relationships and activities of network members.	**Outcomes – Stakeholder group:** Assessing change in behaviour, relationships and activities of parties targeted by network members.
	• establish network web site and public listserv to increase accessibility of developing country-generated content on climate change policy (metrics: amount of traffic to the site); • anchor web site with compendium; all members contribute to compendium analysis of domestic/regional policies; • assist developing country member organizations to participate in COPs (metrics: number of members participating); and • monitor activities for their cumulative "network advantage."	• developing country members working together to aggregate knowledge about climate change, indicated by actively adding content to network web site and compendium; keeping project sections of network web site up to date; • increased input by developing country NGOs to climate change policy process, nationally and internationally, indicated by the number of CCKN member senior staff attending COPs; and • identification of strengths and gaps of the CCKN.	• greater use by policy- and decision-makers of relevant, developing country-produced knowledge on climate change and sustainable development, demonstrated by types of organizations accessing network web site, participating in listserv, interacting with network members at COPs, etc.

Table 11b. Doing things right: Network efficiency.

Steps	Notes from network discussion	
	Activity	**Sample Measures**
Step 5: How are we going to work together?	• Annual network meeting, held concurrently with the annual COP; and • work program consultations.	• number of member organizations represented; level of representation (the principal researcher or a delegate); • number of members actively involved in one or more of the five work programs; and the • number of conference calls held for members in each work program; participation in listserv discussions on work programs.
	Institutional support	• number of member organizations that have signed the governance agreement; and • number which have accepted and provide financial/in-kind support to an IISD intern.
	Financial sustainability	• number of members that prepare project proposals and secure grants for network projects; and • the amount of money secured for network coordination.

Monitoring framework: Progress journals

We have also adapted from outcome mapping the systemized recording of work carried out by members in the network. We have one significant variation on the outcome mapping approach—we do not attempt at this stage to embed any subjective valuation or grading of accomplishments ("expect to see; like to see; love to see") in the progress journal. This is the data gathering stage, not the data evaluation stage. The evaluation of members' work (similar to human resource performance evaluations) is done annually and at the conclusion of project grants.

Quarterly progress journal for each network member

Activities tracked should be consistent with the planning framework; and should not exceed 10 or 12. The journal should be completed quarterly by the member and shared with the network coordinator. A separate journal should be kept for each major work program. This is simply a record of what happened during that quarter and the interesting stories about what is being done, but not an assessment of the work. At the evaluation stage, outcomes for the member and the stakeholders will be derived from the record of progress that has been made by that member and the member's interaction with representatives of the stakeholder group.

Table 12. Hypothetical journal for CCKN member institute for Environment Studies (IVM – Amsterdam) October–December 2000

Project 2 Activities	Member's progress notes	Stakeholder interaction
1. Training workshops	Nothing this quarter.	A follow-up round table was held with developing country negotiators at the beginning of COP-6, to discuss what to look for in the COP-6 round.
2. Handbook, CD Rom	• Handbook drafted; to be called "On behalf of my delegation;" • CSDA handled printing; • IISD handled editing and layout; contracted CD-ROM production; online version put on CCKN web site; • 2,000 printed; and • after COP-6, French and Spanish translations prepared; 1,000 each printed. IVM intern suggested doing a youth version of the book.	• Raúl A. Estrada Oyuela, Ambassador of the Republic of Argentina and Chair of COP-3, agreed to write the foreword to the handbook; • delegates react enthusiastically at COP-6; copies all taken from every venue where displayed; and • requests for French, Spanish translations.
3. Launch at COP-6	Launch organized by IISD and attended by many CCKN members.	

Quarterly Progress Journal for Network Coordinator

Activities tracked should be consistent with the planning framework. The Network Coordinator reviews network-wide activities, including monitoring of network efficiency. Note that the cumulative impact of network activities is reviewed at the annual evaluation. Consequently, there may be very little to record for the network plan on a quarterly basis.

The journal should be completed quarterly and shared with Network members.

Table 13. Hypothetical journal for the CCKN Coordinator, October–December.

The Network Plan	Progress notes	Stakeholder interaction
1. Network web site	Established	
2. COP-6 participation	Senior staff of member organizations attended	Increased level of Southern participation at COP-6.

Network efficiency	Progress notes
1. Network meeting	12 members attended CCKN meeting at COP-6, November 2000
2. Institutional support	Three IISD interns started with network members (Cicero, ENDA and IVM); all three members providing cash and in-kind support to interns
3. Financial sustainability	US AID approached for funding support for Climate Compendium.

Evaluation frameworks

We propose two points at which network activities are evaluated:

1. an *annual evaluation* is needed in order to make adjustments to objectives, work plans, and expected outputs and outcomes. Such adjustments are expected and encouraged when working within results-based management; we have simply described here the process by which the necessary adjustments are identified and agreed to by network members; and
2. a *final evaluation* is usually required by the funder, consistent with the evaluation framework (such as the logical framework analysis) used in the original proposal.

Annual evaluation

It is at this point that we diverge from outcome mapping and draw upon lessons from human resources performance evaluations.

- the network coordinator completes the annual evaluation form for each project, in consultation with the relevant members participating in that project. All forms should be shared across the network; and
- a "level of success" assessment (grading) is introduced.

This process provides the opportunity to adjust activities and expectations, in response to problems encountered and new opportunities which have arisen since the work plan was compiled.

Adjustments to objectives, activities, outputs and anticipated outcomes should then be forwarded to the funder, together with notes on unexpected opportunities and problems (which may correspond to or revise original assumptions and risks noted in a logical framework analysis for the project).

Level of success:

I/P – in progress

D/C – discontinued

1 – did not meet expectations

2 – met expectations

3 – exceeded expectations

Table 14. Hypothetical evaluation for the CCKN, April 2000 – March 2001.

Project 2: Capacity building for climate change negotiators

Activity	Level of success	Outputs
Workshops	3	• Two workshops held: African negotiators workshop, Dakar, Senegal, July 2000: 20 negotiators, from 18 countries attended. Latin American and Caribbean negotiators workshop, Miami, July 2000: 19 negotiators from 13 countries attended. • One follow up roundtable with developing country delegates held at the beginning of COP-6 as a special briefing on what to look for in the COP-6 round. An analysis by IVM of the two workshops was published in *Tiempo* magazine, http://www.cru.uea.ac.uk/tiempo/floor0/archive/issue3637/t3637a6.htm
Handbook, CD ROM, online version	3	English version: 2,000 printed; 1,600 distributed to date; Spanish and French versions: 1000 printed of each, with 700 of each distributed to date
Launch	2	Formal side event planned during COP-6; 60 attended (twice as many as anticipated); most negotiators however were unable to attend as the negotiations were unexpectedly still in session at the time of the event.

Outcomes: Members	Members undertook the project jointly and added significant value to each others' work, without which the workshops and book would not have been as influential. Increased profile for all members involved, which has led to approaches from distance learning specialists to develop online versions of the training program and handbook.
Stories: Members	The workshop led to the idea for the handbook; ENDA reviewed the handbook to ensure that it responded to developing country needs and reflected Southern viewpoints; IISD provided editorial, design and production support to ensure a professional product branded by the network. All English versions of the handbook (book; CD-Rom; online) completed on time for release at COP-6. Increased profile was reflected in the willingness of senior negotiators to become actively engaged in the project. Raúl Estrada, chair of COP-3 (the Kyoto negotiations), agreed to write the foreword to the handbook and to speak at the launch; the chair of the African group of delegates to COP-6, Mamadu Honadia, agreed to speak at the launch; as did Papa Cham, former negotiator for Ghana and currently working with ENDA, one of the CCKN members.
Outcomes: Stakeholders	Increased levels of contact, interaction and trust built with developing country negotiators with each other (through the workshop process) and with the members of the CCKN. Increased demand from negotiators for similar, regular training on both substance and skills, combined with materials like the handbook, in French and Spanish as well as English.
Stories: Stakeholders	The preparatory roundtable with African delegates held at SB-12 in June 2000 was used to gather input and buy-in to the African workshop in July. Consequently the level of representation and participation in that workshop was high. The end of workshop evaluation led to the recommendation that such training should be carried out more regularly and in a similar fashion, combining substance with simulated negotiations. The Latin American workshop focused primarily on negotiation skills and tactics rather than substance. Some participants indicated an interest in having more training in the substance. A follow-up roundtable was therefore held for developing country negotiators at the beginning of COP-6, with a special briefing on what to look for in COP-6. Participation in this roundtable was high. These outcomes were also reflected in the demand for the handbook (published first in English and subsequently (as a result of the demand) in French and Spanish). Delegates at COP-6 were heard to ask where they could find copies; copies made available at various meetings of developing country delegates were all taken almost immediately (an unusual event given the amount of briefing papers and other materials routinely distributed by NGOs and other actors at international negotiations).

Unexpected	The failure to conclude the COP-6 round and the U.S. withdrawal from Kyoto. The IVM intern has begun to develop a similar guide for youth delegates to other major international negotiations, in particular the World Summit for Sustainable Development 2002. Interest has been expressed by negotiators for the desertification convention for similar training and materials for that process.
Adjustments	Plans for replicating the climate change negotiators workshops are on hold until it is clear that the negotiating impasses can be resolved in July 2001. Follow up survey with negotiators in the African and LAC workshops should be conducted, to find out whether they believe their effectiveness at COP-6 was improved as a result of the training; and if so, in what ways was it improved?

Network work plan

Specific Activities	Level of success	Outputs
1. Network web site	2	Web site established, anchored by compendium.
2. Member input to compendium	1	More work needs to be done to approach members for input, and to provide easy means for them to do so.
3. Support member attendance at COPs	3	Senior staff of member organizations attended.

Monitoring the network advantage:

	Note: this section is where the Network Coordinator consolidates the findings from the individual work programs into an assessment of whether the network is fulfilling its potential
Joint value creation:	This is working extremely well at the individual project level, as demonstrated by the success of the negotiators workshops and handbook and the planning for the decentralized renewable energy project. The handbook would not have had the impact it did without the recognition that it was a joint project of the network, legitimized by the contributions of North and South expert institutions. Across the network as a whole, however, joint value aggregation and creation is not as evident. Members are not yet making enough of their own climate change research available so that the network can integrate it on the web site; members are not yet notifying all the members of spin-off products from network activities, such as the *Tiempo* article on the negotiators workshops.

	Members who are not involved directly in one of the projects have not found any other means to add value to the network.
Capacity development across network	There is a growing understanding of Southern perspectives within the network, related particularly to energy as the entry point for the South into the climate change debate. This understanding is strengthening research proposals, training, and other activities. The annual meeting, held during COP, is providing an excellent forum for the exchange of perspectives. Almost all members participate actively in this exchange. More work needs to be done on strengthening individual member communications capacity, to improve their effectiveness within their regions (this includes Northern members).
Links to policy process	Choosing COP as the key policy process with which to connect has led to increased levels of contact, interaction and trust built with key climate change stakeholders in NGO and government communities.
Unexpected	Server traffic not being tracked, therefore unable to get metrics of web site use
Adjustments	A review of the status of members that are not actively involved in projects may need to be carried out.

Table 15. Hypothetical annual evaluation for the CCKN network efficiency component, April 2000 – March 2001.

Network efficiency	Level of success	Comments
Meetings	3	12 out of 14 members attended the network meeting at COP-6, The Hague.
Institutional support IISD	2	14 members have signed the governance agreement; Three members are supporting an intern; CSDA would like to host an intern in 2001–02.
Financial sustainability	3	Core funding for the network from IDRC and CIDA leveraged additional funding for the capacity building project, from Norway's Royal Ministry of Foreign Affairs and Canada's Department of Foreign Affairs and International Trade.
Unexpected		U.S. withdrawal from Kyoto has put U.S. funding for the compendium in 2001–02 on hold.
Adjustments		Compendium project on hold until funding confirmed or new funding secured. Funding proposals will be prepared to transfer the negotiators workshop methodology to the desertification arena.

Evaluation report to funder at end of grant

This report should be completed by the network coordinator and circulated to members for comment, prior to submission to the funder. Not all funders require reporting against methodologies such as results-based management and logical framework analysis. For those that do, we have shown below how our approach corresponds to the relevant sections in RBM and LFA.

Sample final evaluation framework

Grading overall:

1 – Did not meet expectations

2 – Met expectations

3 – Exceeded expectations

Network effectiveness: This section corresponds to results-based management (RBM) development results		
Overall network goals and objectives: what did we think success might look like for the network and did we achieve that? General observations		
Network advantage summary	**Level of success**	**Comments** This section corresponds to LFA purpose and points towards the likelihood of contributing in a positive way towards the longer term LFA goal.
Engagement of stakeholders in policy process and action		
Joint value creation		
Capacity development		
Specific Projects 1 (2, 3)		
Activities; cumulative outputs	**Level of success**	**Comments** This section corresponds to Logical Framework Analysis (LFA) outputs.
Cumulative outcomes: Network members		This section corresponds to LFA purpose.
Cumulative outcomes: Stakeholder group		This section corresponds to LFA purpose and points towards the likelihood of contributing in a positive way towards the longer term LFA goal.

Network efficiency: This section maps to RBM operational results		
Cumulative activities	**Level of success**	**Comments**

Further research

The frameworks we have proposed are experimental. We have drawn from our experience with web site traffic analysis, with networks and project evaluation in order to create frameworks which we think might provide us with useful information, but we have yet to test these systematically across our own networks and alliances. We are in the process now of putting the planning and monitoring frameworks into place for the second phases of the Climate Change Knowledge Network and the Trade Knowledge Network. We also anticipate that we will be able to promote these frameworks to other networks of which we are members, including the International Institute for Environment and Development's Regional International Networking Group (the RING). We will also use the evaluation framework in our retrospective look at the two phases of the Sustainable Development Communications Network.

Earlier, we stated that the rationale for investing in knowledge management and knowledge networks:

- filling the knowledge gaps that inhibit policy development for sustainable development;
- generating recommendations that will fast track innovation for sustainability;
- resolving current frustrations with inadequate or inappropriate policy development and implementation; and
- learning from each other across sectors and regions about best practices,

has been more than adequately explored by others.[93] What we do not know yet is how to monitor and evaluate whether this investment is paying dividends in current and emerging knowledge networks.

Over the next two to three years, IISD will be developing a research program to explore the "network advantage" further. We will be seeking answers to the following questions:

- Can a network determine what changes it has effected through its research and communications work? Will our methodology help networks not only to assess individual activities, but provide some means for identifying changes as a result of its combination of efforts?

- Can network coordinators demonstrate to their own members that it is worth the institutional investment of time and effort in order to sustain network momentum over the long term?

We will also be looking carefully at questions of network efficiency. Are there standard practices for networks, as much as there are standard practices for human resources management, and can we identify these through improved performance evaluation of networks? Ultimately, can we answer the question, whether it is better in the end for a funder to give $200,000 to each of five organizations to carry out research on a given issue, rather than $1 million to a formal network of five organizations?

Our research program will have a number of components:

- Retrospective analysis: we will look at evaluations of older networks; interview network organizers and members, and cast the evaluation into our framework, to see whether we can demonstrate consistent achievement of the network advantage;
- Analysis of current projects: we will put our planning, monitoring and evaluation frameworks in place for IISD's networks and alliances, to see whether we can achieve some consistency in identifying and cumulating our successes; and
- Comparative analysis: We will attempt to compare similar projects being conducted by one or two networks, and by several independent institutions, to see whether we can validate our assumptions that networks do operate more efficiency and effectively than single source research efforts.

We know that there will be some major challenges to overcome in promoting our approach to network evaluation. Network members tend to view evaluation as the responsibility of the member that received the grant for the project or network; and the network managers tend to view evaluation as a task that can wait until the funder requires a report. We need to effect at least one significant behavioural change with our research: that network members and managers will begin to monitor their work more regularly, to see whether their collaboration is in fact leading to better-informed research results, new knowledge and real influence.

Endnotes

91 Anderson, Scott *et al. Tools for assessing web site usage.* IISD Working Paper, (Winnipeg: IISD, 2000).

92 We have adopted these characteristics from M. Gladwell, *The Tipping Point: How little things can make a big difference* (Boston: Little, Brown, 2000). Mavens are the research experts; connectors are those with connections to decision-makers; salespeople are those with the ability to craft and communicate messages. Selection of members with reference to these characteristics is discussed in Chapter 4.

93 Creech. *Strategic Intentions*, p. 24.